The Madness of Modern Families

Annie Ashworth and Meg Sanders

The Madness
of Modern Families

HODDER &
STOUGHTON

Copyright © 2006 by Wordright Limited

Illustrations by Claire Clements/Miekeljohn

First published in Great Britain in 2006 by Hodder & Stoughton
A division of Hodder Headline

A Maverick Production for BBC. Licensed by RDF Rights.

The right of Annie Ashworth and Meg Sanders to be identified
as the Author of the Work has been asserted by them in
accordance with the Copyright, Designs and Patents Act 1988.

A Hodder & Stoughton Book

2

The names and identities of the people
quoted in this book have been changed.

A CIP catalogue record for this title is available from the British Library

ISBN 978 0 340 92341 3
ISBN 0 340 92341 5

Typeset in Sabon by Hewer Text UK Ltd, Edinburgh
Printed and bound by Clays Ltd, St Ives plc

Hodder Headline's policy is to use papers that are natural, renewable
and recyclable products and made from wood grown in sustainable
forests. The logging and manufacturing processes are expected to
conform to the environmental regulations of the country of origin.

Hodder & Stoughton Ltd
A division of Hodder Headline
338 Euston Road
London NW1 3BH

To our wonderful children,
who have proved that madness is inherited.
We got it from you.

Contents

Once Upon a Time . . .

The sun is setting at the end of another lovely day. The children are singing together in the back of the car and giggling, planning the make-believe game they are going to play when they get home. You all unload the shopping they helped you choose at the village shop – Oh, how Lizzie loves those little organic yoghurts and of course Jamie wants broccoli with his steamed fish tonight – and your teenage son helps you put it all away in the cupboard before making you a cup of tea and going off to do his homework. You put on your pinnie, ready to make a crumble for pudding from the apples from the orchard, and smile to yourself, secure in the knowledge that your husband will pull up on the drive any minute and you can share the happy stories of your day.

Yeah. As if . . . In reality, you have just schlepped round the chaotic out-of-town supermarket and frantically crammed in over-priced organic vegetables and the pizza you know you shouldn't have bought but did anyway because it's quicker, and thrown them in the back of the car along with the child who has whinged the whole way round the supermarket pestering you for a packet of bubble gum, which of course you gave in to. Then you screeched out of the car park in your 4 x 4 which you bought because you read it was the safest means of transport for children and pulled up outside school for the third time that day to collect a stroppy thirteen-year-old who is covered in mud and hungry and spurns the apple crisps you offer shouting that he wants a Mars Bar, then goes on the computer instead of getting washed and on with his homework while you try to find room in the fridge for the food and find your daughter's ballet shoes because in ten minutes you have to leave for a class which you have read is good for her balance and posture, while chivvying up your ten-year-old who doesn't want to go to karate even though he nagged you about getting him in and sat on the waiting list for three months before a place came up and you bought the uniform. Your husband calls to say he's going to be late after all and the dog is sick on the carpet and your mother is coming over for lunch tomorrow, then the office email to say that report you aim to deliver on Monday has to be done for tomorrow or they'll lose the client.

That, dear reader, is modern family life. A catastrophe of optimism over the grim reality of 'parenting'.

The word 'parenting'. Now what exactly is that all about? I parent, you parent, he parents . . . (well, usually she, actually). Since when did 'parenting' become a verb? It is no coincidence that it appeared in the lexicon about the same time as networking, down-shifting, interfacing and other management-ese 'ings' because it has suddenly become a profession. A career. Something on the CV to be taken ever so seriously.

Ask your parents if they ever used the word 'parenting' and they will probably snort with laughter (they laugh at everything else we do). They were our mums and dads, they didn't do *parenting*. Any more than they *incentivised*, or had *interpersonal solutions*. No, parenting is a late twentieth-century phenomenon like yuppiedom and up-ward mobility. They may have invented sex in the sixties, but we invented parenting. It's not even a skill any more – it's a science. We know that because someone called Dr Margot Sunderland has written a book with that very title.

Why has this happened? The problem is there isn't any one single answer. Just look at the world we are living in, for heaven's sake. It's about as straightforward as trying to put a nappy on an octopus. Look at us: you can send an email to Costa Rica in seconds, but you can't drive more than 10 mph round the Hanger Lane gyratory on a Monday morning. People are on waiting lists for hip replacements and handbags. Footballers are paid the equivalent GDP of a small African country to wear a certain brand of hat. We have machines that cook pizza in seconds and yet we get stressed about leisure. We even use words like 'leisure'. On TV we watch total strangers locked in a house or stranded on an island together and call it entertainment.

The paradoxes are enough to scramble your brain. It's a mad world; no wonder we are all mixed up. No wonder what was once the most natural thing in the world – raising a family – sends us into a frenzy of self-doubt. We are surrounded by an information superhighway, but it seems to contradict itself all the time. And everywhere is spin, spin, spin that creates a tyranny of fear.

You want to raise a family that is happy and thriving, but have to do this in a world where it has become harder and harder. So we invented the concept of 'parenting' because we had to give it a name. It couldn't be something that just happens. If we name it, we can control it and have theories about it, and talk about it. Is it a result of our own upbringing? Doubt it – it all seemed a heck of a lot easier when you got two shillings pocket money and were in bed by eight thirty. We didn't get sent to podiatrists, homeopaths and cranial osteopaths because we weren't picked for the netball team. Nor did our mums and dads track us with GPS systems like criminals.

The only mistake they made was to launch us into a world where we expect to be happy and perfect, because we have been told we could be.

Even though our rational heads know it is nonsense and all we need to be is *good enough*, we still find ourselves buying into this ideal. We are held to ransom by the headline writers and cover line writers of magazines. Take titles like *Green Parents* which had a letter from the editor, pictured sitting with her two rosy-cheeked children on a hay bale, that goes on about how she chose the 'natural birth and gentle mothering approach for her daughters'. We read about contributors whose favourite place in the world is their kitchen because 'each time I put the kettle on I'm standing in the spot where I gave birth'. And we ask ourselves:

why am I reading this smug pap, but know it's because we picked up the magazine like a brainwashed automaton lured by the cover line: 'Ethical Chocolate – Would You Let Your Children Eat Anything Else?'

Unable to break away, our eyes wander back to the news-stand and any one of the squillion parenting magazines there to torment us. 'How to be happy', says one. 'Your toddler – how to make the most of quality time', crows another. 'Is your baby too fat/too thin/too tall/too stupid?' 'How hopeless are you? Try our quiz and find out!' 'Working? You terrible mother, how could you?' 'Be a more successful parent'. Okay, we made some up, but bet you can't work out which we didn't.

There's the pressure: I must succeed. I must make them happy. They must be perfect. And I must make it look as easy as a walk in the park, the swings and slides of which have been passed by Health and Safety.

We realised, when we were writing our novels, *Goodbye, Jimmy Choo, Warnings of Gales,* and *The Xmas Factor*, that we were starting to explore the craziness of these new modern families – creating characters who were trying desperately to juggle everything and be brilliant at all of it. But it was only when we started this book that we realised how all-pervasively mad the modern family has become. In fact, the weirdest part was getting people to own up to their vulnerability and, on occasion, lunacy. They knew exactly what we were getting at – and always knew someone else who'd done something really barking – but were still reluctant to admit they were struggling to get it right themselves. 'Don't quote me!' squealed a lot of people, as if they were owning up to something illegal or perverted.

Penny Wilson was the co-founder of a regrettably short-lived magazine called *Wipe*, intended to be the antidote to self-congratulatory, patronising parenting magazines, with frank articles with headlines like 'Sex? I remember that'. Tell it like it is, was the motto. The response to its launch was massive. 'We were inundated with letters from people,' says Penny, 'all saying, "Thank God! Thank you for being honest." '

How odd is that? The biggest requirement of being a parent these days seems to be the ability to be a masterful liar. We have to pretend that we are fulfilled, that we aren't tired, that the baby is sleeping, and we manage seven orgasms a week. Life has become like some gingham-pinnied Doris Day fantasy – oh, and in your spare time you are chief executive of a multinational corporation. Or if you aren't, you probably have an MBA in stay-at-home motherhood.

Remember the heroine of Allison Pearson's novel *I Don't Know How She Does It* who systematically distresses mince pies so people will think she has made them? It wasn't enough to say, 'I have a high-powered, full-time job – sorry, no time for baking.' She *had* to fake it.

The question is always in our heads. Am I failing? Am I doing it right? Small wonder when our role model is the Tom Cruise School of Parenting where celebs buy their own ultrasound machines. And this is held up as a good thing?

We have all been sucked into this charade – even people we once thought sane. But hey, sisters and brothers! It's time to stand up and say, 'We are Mad Modern Parents, with Mad Modern Families, and now we'd like to go and have a little nap please. Wake us when it's all over.'

I

Welcome to Planet Parenting . . .

. . . A world you never even thought about until you crash-landed here. Beware, the air is thin and the day much longer than you are used to. As in all worlds there are tribes here, some friendlier than others, but as sure as ovaries is ovaries, you will be sucked in to one of them. Or worse, you might take on the characteristics of several.

Craft Mummy

Her house is a chaotic mess of creativity where good taste and wedding present Bridgewater china on the kitchen dresser have been buried beneath works of art fashioned from fusilli pasta and Mexican dough. A moth-eared Father's Day card from a couple of years back, the 'I Love You' formed from screwed-up bits of yellow tissue paper and glued, takes pride of place. It's the family's year catalogued in craft.

Pinned to the fridge by a cheeky magnet will be a tatty piece of paper on which is scribbled the recipe for home-made playdough, gleaned from a friend at nursery, and in a big plastic box from B&Q will be crammed every last bit of string, old Christmas cards or interesting piece of fluffy fabric that has been squirrelled away until friends of her daughter's come over to tea. Then they will be offered home-made biscuits, misshapen but charming, the packet of Haribo your child arrived with secreted away in the top of a cupboard, and the art fest will begin.

Craft Mum runs herself ragged mopping up spilt PVA, because the warm conviction she has deep inside that creative time is wholly good does not completely quash her terror of red and blue finger marks all over the Farrow & Balled walls. Her real intention is to make you feel woefully inadequate because all you will have time for, on a return fixture, will be a trip to the park and a Mr Whippy. Enough to make you feel like sniffing Pritt stick. As you leave with your paint-covered child, Craft Mummy will carefully hand you a collage of leaves and grasses that is 'not quite dry'.

It will be immediately sat on by the dog in the back of the car.

Too Posh to Push Parents

For Sarah, pregnancy is a wonderful excuse to go shopping. Since the moment she squealed the exciting news to all her girlfriends – not forgetting to drop in that it had been conceived in the Maldives – she has been in a credit card-flashing frenzy, securing a stash of Elle McPherson maternity underwear and plundering the rails in Bumpsville and Blossom. The only fly in Sarah's ointment is that Prada don't do a range. Determined that, not for one second, will she look frumpy pre or post partum – did you *see* those pictures of Britney in *Hello!*? – she wears her bump as if it were a designer accessory, dreamily rubbing in Japanese Camellia Oil to keep those pesky stretch marks at bay, and has acquired an air whereby she appears to float in an aura of fragile femininity; if Gwyneth can do it, so can she. She takes life gently, does a bit more shopping and meets the girls in Beauchamp Place for something light for lunch (though she could murder a bag of chips).

Truth be known though, Sarah has been flicking quickly past the bits in the baby book about the actual *birth* – it can't really be that gross can it? – which is why, as they are just out of the catchment area for the Chelsea & Westminster, she has persuaded husband Nick to stump up for a private delivery. The hospital literature makes it sound more like a hotel (she likes the words 'ensuite' and 'deluxe') and it even does à la carte. Of course it will all be lovingly recorded on camcorder and announced in *The Times*, though friends will be able to see a picture of the baby via the web thanks to the hospital's picture posting system. Her mother, who drops by occasionally to visit her expanding daughter, wafting Dior as she goes, will approve, though of course in her day they 'lay in'.

Sarah also finds the consultant's soothing words about 'a section if we feel it is necessary' very reassuring. It will fit in nicely around Nick's work schedule and what does it matter if she takes a bit longer to recover? She'd rather that than an episiotomy – yeuch! – and the maternity nurse starts the moment they get home, so why worry?

Everyone agrees that it's sensible to give the baby the best possible start in life, and, anyway, it's already down for the best schools, so that's the whole thing sorted.

For Sarah, motherhood was a wonderful
excuse to go shopping.

The Sensitive Man

Chris has been sick with nerves since the moment, twelve months ago, Abby told him the pregnancy test was positive. Obviously he was proud as hell, relieved that he wasn't firing blanks because he couldn't have borne being told to 'provide a sample' at a clinic, but a lifetime of responsibility, school fees and insurance policies looms ahead. During the pregnancy he was in awe and admiration of Abby as she blossomed and swelled, and he remembered to listen attentively to all the details of her antenatal visits. He even sat through NCT classes while the instructor stuffed a purple-haired troll enthusiastically through a plastic pelvis in the absence of a doll to demonstrate the 'birth journey'. Now that Freddie has come into the world, Chris's life has changed for ever and having the little mite around has helped him forget the twenty hours of labour torture. He'd been told rubbing Abby's back was a good idea, so why did she tell him to bugger off? Somewhere a voice tells him that pacing the corridors with a cigar would have been preferable but he would rather have eaten the placenta than admit it.

He took his allocated paternity leave, is rather proud of the fact that he's an expert on the contents of each nappy (and he changes as many as he can), and nods sympathetically when regaled about the trials of lactation. More supportive than a nursing bra, he can bore for Europe at kitchen supper parties with other new parents, as the wives breastfeed shamelessly at the table, and finds common ground with the other men about the pros and cons of different buggies, knowing exactly which one fits best into an Audi.

But deep down he's panic-stricken that he's lost his wife for good and is desperate for a Saturday morning shag like the good old days. Meanwhile, he's wanking for Britain.

Eco Mummy

There's a bit of a funny smell in Belinda's house, but you don't really want to ask. Is it the ever-present bucket of nappies soaking in the corner or the jam jar of alfalfa sprouts, left a bit too long on the windowsill? Take care not to accept a drink. She'll pass you a mug of Barleycup with several rings still in evidence – she'd never dream of having a dishwasher cos of the impact on the environment – but if you are quick you can tip it into the weeping fig. Little Jerome, gurgling happily in his sustainable wood highchair, doesn't care that all his unbleached cotton romper suits are now a lighter shade of grey – no optical whiteners in this house, thank you very much.

But his older sisters have realised something's up. Desperate for invitations to houses where they get Jaffa Cakes and can watch TV, they try to make new friends by offering the wholemeal contents of their lunchbox, but to no avail. Their classmates turn up their noses at bio-dynamic felafel and organic mushroom pâté. Belinda's offspring – home deliveries every one (it's a wonder they didn't name the youngest Ocado) – live in constant hope of an invitation to a McDonald's party, but know that if one came their way they wouldn't be allowed to go.

Obsessive to the point of mania, Belinda is determined that she will single-handedly make the world a better place for her children by driving a thirty-mile round trip to the only recycling plant that takes Tetrapaks.

As you leave, picking your way out through the hallway cluttered with bikes, overflowing bags on their way to the charity shop and the box of organic veg delivered weekly, you feel completely traumatised at the thought of your carbon footprint and the terrible harm you've done your children by allowing them to have drinks from plastic bottles. And who could have imagined there were so many pesticides in a carton of apple juice? Belinda's clear-eyed zeal and fresh-faced evangelism has you in a frenzy of self-doubt. You go home and empty your cupboards of all the cleaning products that actually work – then have to buy in a new stock when that odd smell you detected round her house starts to pervade the atmosphere of your kitchen too.

The Foodie Parent

Richard and Sophie's kitchen is a shrine to the senses and a temple to the finest food the world can provide. Their children know it, your children know it. In fact, everyone knows it, because the Foodies keep telling them so.

No ingredient is too recherché for the family. Sophie consumes cookbooks like most people do novels and is on the phone to Valvona & Crolla weekly. Each meal is a 'menu gastronomique' with a perfect balance of little courses, each seasoned to perfection. On the table at mealtimes are Halen Môn salt crystals, wasabi (which your child thought was snot), and vinaigrette (made with their home-brewed vinegar, using a matrix they picked up in northern Italy, donchaknow).

Their children's gourmet palates have been developed since before they entered Little Sod's Nursery. No fish fingers in this establishment! Sophie's idea of fast food is seared scallops. Thanks to intensive highchair training in 'super little places' on foodie pilgrimages through Europe, Foodie kids can identify a Maris Piper from a Pink Fir Apple at a single bite – although they've never been near a chip. Their lunchboxes would have Michel Roux in tears of envy. The only chocolate they've ever tasted is Valrhona. Is there any other kind?

When you tremulously offer the Foodie kids pasta on a play date, they ask you to be more specific: linguine? Eliche? Penne rigate? They'll reject the shop-bought pesto, cos it's not made with extra virgin olive oil, but they wouldn't mind tapenade. You're frantically searching the larder, wondering if Marmite would do, when salvation comes in the unexpected form of a bag of Cheesy Wotsits. You tell them they're Japanese rice crackers and they munch away contentedly.

Quality Time Mum

Probably working in some high-powered job she refuses to give up (it took her so long to get there), Rebecca is racked with guilt. About everything – all the time. At work for not being at home, at home for not being at work. She virtually gave birth in her lunch hour, having finished off a presentation in the early stages of labour before taking a taxi to the hospital. She chose a place that provided a fax machine and broadband in every room. With an epidural, she could carry on with phone calls to Frankfurt until the midwife forcibly removed the handset from her grip.

She was back at work within a week, half the time spent crying out the hormones in the lavs and the other half trying to staunch the flow of breast milk on her Ungaro silk shirt. She made Nicola Horlick look like a slacker. Her permanently knackered three-year-old, who's kept awake by the nanny until 'Mummy gets home' has come to dread these twenty-minute intensive fairy cake-baking sessions with her mother, a virtual stranger who has a phone glued to her ear talking to the office. Rebecca knows she is gushing every time she comes home (late) to make up for lost time, yet screeches in on sports day at the last minute and pretends she saw her daughter come fifth in the egg and spoon. Half her salary goes on the nanny but they both know the family couldn't survive without her.

She has to keep everyone happy, so Saturday mornings are 'Daddy and Mummy time' – while CBBC babysits – then she makes herself feel better by meeting colleagues with children for a power Sunday brunch on Upper Street; but 'it's a treat for the kids, isn't it?' She collapses into bed at the end of each day, thanking her lucky stars for the fact that she has so many choices available in her life. I am woman – hear me snore!

Helicopter Mum

What's that strange whirring noise that accompanies little Hector wherever he goes? Why, it's Tamsin, his mummy, hovering at a safe distance, far enough away to allow him to interact, at least a little, with other people, yet close enough to swoop should she judge it necessary. Always ready with an opinion, an answer, a wet-wipe or a snack, she's as connected to him now as she was by the umbilicus, and as crucial to his wellbeing, or so she would have you (and him) think.

He's never quite on his own, Hector, although Tamsin did once leave him with the trusted Mrs Arkle who cleans - while she went upstairs to change. At five he has yet to speak because Tamsin does it for him. She refers to him as 'We', as in, 'Oh, no, we never have butter on our bread,' or, 'We had a bit of a late night, I'm afraid, so we might be a wee bit grumpy today.'

Tamsin is particularly noticeable at parties, where she enters like an avenging Health and Safety Officer to scan the room for potential hazards. Of course she always stays, offering to help. How kind, how thoughtful, you think, until you notice that the only thing she's interested in helping with is Hector. She ignores any other child's request for juice, takes over refereeing Musical Statues to make sure he wins and refuses to help with the washing up, because she can't actually see him from the kitchen.

At school, she resorts to helping in class so she can keep an eye. At the playground on Saturdays she shadows his progress on the equipment, her car keys clenched in her hand, her knuckles white, just in case they have to dash to A&E. Don't bother trying to engage her in conversation. She's constantly looking over your shoulder to check on his status and won't hear a word you say. If you'd really like to speak to her, go and chat to Hector. She'll be there like a shot, ready and eager to respond.

Taxi Driver

The world looks a better place from an SUV. And with everything she needs stashed away in that copious glove box, Anne secretly relishes her driving hours although, with all the eye-rolling and tutting she does, you'd never guess. Between 8.07 and 8.52 precisely she braves the morning traffic, her route honed to perfection, as she transports William and Catriona, plus all their paraphernalia, to their respective schools, chanting tables, conjugating French verbs and handing out wet wipes to remove all traces of breakfast on the move, all at breakneck speed.

The rest of the day feels oddly flat, although, of course, she has to shop to restock the glove box/larder (the menu limited to foodstuffs you can hoover up with a Dustbuster), and tries to meet up with friends to compare their packed schedules in case they can lift-share. (The hidden agenda is finding out if anyone has discovered a new and more interesting activity she should be plugging into.) Then from 3.17 until whenever, she swerves the kids from one improving activity to the next, getting home just in time for a quick bath before bed.

Anne has, so far, resisted in-car DVDs but at least the

kids would be able to watch *Muzzy*, still in its wrapping and gathering dust at home, and it would be a good use of driving time. Shame she has to pick them up early from pottery so as to make sure they only miss the first five minutes of tai kwando, but there's no other way. Thank heavens she did that chart on the computer so she can work out which of the many sports bags she has to stow on which day.

The children, exhausted but resigned, change their clothes as required in the back. All they really want is to cuddle up in the sitting room and watch *Blue Peter* once in a while so they can join in the conversation at school, and eat shepherd's pie at the kitchen table with a real knife and fork.

Double-parked outside the leisure centre, Anne is free, for twenty-five minutes at least, to flick through *Vogue*. It's a punishing schedule for her. Still – when you have such gifted children – there really is no choice . . .

The 'Been There Done That'

Jenny has climbed the foothills of babies and toddlers, negotiated the glaciers of the tween years, cramponed and ice-picked her way up the north face of teenagers and has reached the summit. From the privileged position of one who has children for whom A levels are a distant memory, she looks down on you as you battle the challenges below. A bit like an older sister, she listens with a slight smile as you rant and rail about recalcitrant behaviour, common entrance or incompetent teachers, and you take her smile for support and sympathy. In reality it is wry and knowing, even a tad patronising. She nods reassuringly, 'it's only a phase', which is as helpful as telling someone in the middle of root canal work 'it'll soon be over', then utters those magnificent words that fill your heart with dread: 'This is nothing. Just you wait.'

Thousands of miles ahead of you on the parenting trail, Jenny can discuss GCSE options and theory driving tests, knowing you will have no comprehension of what she is talking about. She's an expert on gap years and UCAS forms – it's all so different now, you know – can tell you why geography is better at Loughborough than Newcastle and refers to them all as 'uni'. When you visit for coffee she struggles to find a biscuit suitable for your toddler, and leaps up with, 'Don't touch that, sweetheart,' as he lunges for her son's mobile phone. Said son then strolls in and picks up the keys to the Mini Cooper from the table. Do children really get that big?

Jenny, who dresses a bit like your mother, smiles indulgently but don't be fooled. All that nonchalance hides a ball of anxiety, but she'll never admit how easy early parenting is compared to the horrors of having children who are no longer an 'een' and who are about to flee the nest and, ergo, her clutches.

Designer Parents

Function follows form for Giles and Daisy. Every purchase, every item in the house is an *homage* to their highly developed aesthetic taste – and that goes for the baby stuff too. It was a bit of a shock, that first trip round Mothercare. All that plastic! All that colour! It seemed there was just no way you could make a baby minimalist!

Things have moved on a bit now, thank goodness. Now that babies are a recognised fashion accessory, DPs are far better catered for. From the Bill Amberg papoose to the huge Bugaboo, there's plenty to satisfy their retail longings. Gracious, Armani even do a baby range. With cashmere bootees from Brora and Alice Temperley rompers, they'll match Mummy's cardi and frock beautifully. Daisy can use the kids as an excuse to visit all her fave shops and there's always a chance you'll bump into little Apple, or Lila with nanny in tow, or even (oh, joy) their mummies, while you're browsing the racks.

The problems may arise when the kids start to assert their own taste – sadly, their choice of telly programmes doesn't bode well. There's no way you could ever call a Boobah chic, even in an ironic way, and as for *Balamory* . . . Overalls? I don't think so!

The PTA Parent

Ever since she was chair of the Junior Common Room at UEA, Mandy has been able to smell a committee at five hundred yards and she can't resist being *involved*. Her motivation this time, though, is that she is in awe of Ben's teachers – the closed staffroom door making it no more accessible now than when she was at school – and she feels it's so important to be a key player in school life.

She has made certain inroads by always making herself

available to accompany school trips and positioning herself next to the form teacher on the coach, but the woman remained irritatingly unresponsive to leading questions about Ben's progress, even though Mandy bought her coffee in the science museum café!

She's pretty pleased that the head now calls her by her first name, achieved thanks to her persistence in signing herself that way on emails to him, but she can't help thinking that, by joining in the fund-raising for new computers, she'll cement the relationship even further. The fact that she's single-handedly organising the Auction of Promises supper might be valuable when Mr Cafferty marks Ben's Victorians project. He's bound to be wowed by the postcards they've stuck in which shows they did the museums and didn't just Google it.

Mandy is always there early for collection at 3.15 so she can collar people and ask them to help with raffle tickets, but they all seem to be deep in conversations or have to rush away. Well, she complains to the mother of Ben's best friend as they wrap gel pens for the tombola, they'll never raise the necessary funds flogging a couple of fairy cakes at the school fête. Someone has to be committed. They'll have her to thank, though, when there're two lovely new computers in the library.

Touchline Dad

Greg looks forward to Sunday morning mini rugby with mixed emotions. William takes a bit of persuading, especially when it's zero degrees outside, but Greg's enormous investment in 'battle gear' shoulder pads and a fluorescent green gum shield was a worthwhile bribe just to see the lad jog out on to the pitch in his strip.

Greg's enthusiasm is greater than the quality of his own schoolboy rugby, as he barely scraped the thirds – though, as he recalls, it was a particularly good year group for second row players – but time has healed the wound and now he invests all his boyhood ambitions in young William. Sport at St Lawrence School is derisory, and the only option anyway is football which everyone knows is for wusses, so minis on the Sabbath it is.

The volume at which he bellows 'Get stuck in, son!' makes one wonder just what decibels he could reach during a nail-biting Calcutta Cup clash at Twickenham, but Greg keeps up the verbal pressure. You just never know: a county talent-scout may be lurking by the corner flag. William, at once both confused and embarrassed, looks across at his Barbour-wrapped father on the touch-line, because he is nowhere near the ball anyway. Nor does he intend to be, because it hurts, his legs have turned blue and he can't feel the ends of his fingers.

His father's verve is equalled if not surpassed by his mother's, who sits at the end of the pool at swimming galas and times his backstroke on the stopwatch facility on her mobile, explaining away his poor performance to others with excuses about late nights and being 'under the weather'. Why can't she see he's never going to be quicker than Henry, who must have webbed feet, and who cares anyway? William just wants to go home and play with his Lego.

William is six.

'Come on son, you'll never get to Twickenham that way!'

Crop Top Mum

Lou got her figure back really fast after pregnancy – well, never lost it, actually – and, boy, does she let everyone else know! It's hard work staying so hot, but worth it because it means she and her daughter are more like sisters – bezzie m8s. And that's got to be good – right? Her signature crop top, worn whatever the weather, also reveals her belly button piercing, much to her eleven-year-old, Laura's, embarrassment, but it was the price that had to be paid for being allowed to get her ears pierced. Now Laura just has to convince her mum that low-slung trousers are so *yesterday*, and that long sweaters are in.

Lou and Laura have always been on first-name terms – because they really respect each other as individuals. That doesn't stop Lou from appropriating all her daughter's slang, textese, dance moves and tastes in music. She also insists on chatting to her friends and wants them all to feel really at home in her house, all the better to spy on what they're wearing and copy it. Her role model is Peaches Geldof.

When Lou offered to take Laura and all her mates to see Robbie as a birthday treat, who was up at the front, arms in the air, singing while Laura cringed, scarlet with humiliation, in the loos? Your daughter, by contrast, thinks Lou's really cool and demands to know why you don't take more care of yourself.

You always feel about a hundred when you go to Lou's house to pick up your daughter. It seems like a permanent sleepover party there, with Lou serving up bowl after bowl of popcorn, watching DVDs with the girls. Still, at least your daughter doesn't keep you waiting. In fact, she's desperate to leave once you appear because you're so drab, and she doesn't want Lou to spot your awful old M&S Footglove shoes and haggard, make-up-free face.

The Tate Parent

India was a late and unexpected blessing in Jane and Harry's marriage. She is the most perfect creature they could imagine and she never tries their infinite patience. Granted, the adjustment has been, well, frankly immense and Harry has had to put a lock on his study door since the day she crawled in there and shredded his notes for Monday's lecture on Eastern European economics. But she coped very well with last year's trip to Peru and looked like a native in her little papoose on Jane's back.

Jane is frankly terrified of her daughter, especially when Harry goes off to work in the college department that also used to be the centre of her world until she had to give it all up – a nanny? Unthinkable! – and she is faced with the long day ahead. She looks at her daughter's faintly menacing expression as she chews on a wholemeal crust in her highchair. Getting her down will be not unlike unleashing the dogs of war, and Jane has spent hours of reasoned bargaining with promises of extra *Tickabilla* if she will only stop terrorising the cat.

India will almost inevitably be artistic given the family genes on both sides, and no doubt she will absorb culture by osmosis, but there's no harm in helping nature along.

Hence the family days out to significant art galleries and museums. Harry, in a voice loud enough to benefit anyone else standing close by, crouches down beside India in her buggy and explains, in the simplest terms he can, the influences behind Vorticism. At twenty-four months, India is mad as hell at being strapped in so whines and twists her body in protest. Her parents, keen that she should be able to express herself, release her and watch with glee as she waddles towards the Rachel Whiteread installation. What a glorious sight to see their precious daughter captivated by such a profound artistic statement! They retire shortly afterwards for refreshment in the café, exhausted by attempts to stop her clambering all over it.

Perhaps, Jane wonders as she sips her green tea, the Eden Project might engage her more.

The Mother of All Teenagers

Lucy has dealt with more confrontation and negotiation in the last twenty-four hours than Kofi Annan has ever had to contend with. She has tried the softly, softly approach and has now got as far as 'because I say so', but has fallen short of raising her voice even further because if that doesn't work, she'll have exhausted her arsenal.

Tash remains resolute. Natasha seemed such a pretty name to choose for their daughter, and seemed to suit so well the biddable little thing who used to put her arms around her mother's neck and tell her she loved her to the moon and back. It doesn't seem to suit this . . . this alien standing here in the kitchen, her jeans hugging bony hips, her arms folded, her face as hard as nails, informing her mother that it is totally unreasonable not to let her stay over at the house of a friend of a friend of her mate Georgie's, the address of which is uncertain. Lucy would love Alan to be here to help, but her husband is totally at a loss to understand this oestrogen-driven fifteen-year-old who occupies their house like a malign wraith, and he finds sales meetings at the office a blessed relief.

Unsure whether she should be suggesting the Pill, but worried it might be planting the wrong message in Tash's head, Lucy tries very hard not to nag with questions, knowing it's the quickest way to alienate her daughter. During the day, however, she can't resist going through her room, on the pretext of tidying it, and picks up the scantiest of knickers from the floor, discarded with her FCUK T-shirts, and wonders, with a large dose of panic, just who they are intended to attract. This all seems light years away from the Laura Ashley dresses and innocent kisses of *her* far-off teenage years.

The only thing Lucy and her daughter have in common is that they both think the mobile phone is the greatest invention since penicillin. For Tash it's a means of directing her social life and confirming to her friends that her mother too is totally 'sad'. For Lucy it's a substitute umbilical cord – Tash can't ignore a 'where ru?' text message, can she? – but it's a mixed blessing at 3 a.m.: Oh, God, why hasn't she replied?

2

Babies: Let's Start at the Very Beginning

Obviously a child is the basic accessory we need to qualify as a parent. That's nothing new; parents have been having children for years. But these days becoming a parent suddenly needs to fit in to some *grand scheme*. A life plan. It's all very thought through and deliberate. It's one of the many things we hope to achieve before we turn forty. Like doing a parachute jump, or buying a BMW.

The trouble is, for women at least, the scheduling starts just about the time we choose our A levels.

Preconceptions

Here's how it seems to go: we choose a career path and hurtle along it, then, once we've established ourselves and got the company pension, we form a partnership with someone who shares our vision and set up a base that reflects our corporate beliefs. After that expansion seems the logical thing to do. Yes, it's a serious project, doing the baby thing, but with the right research and plenty of investment, eminently doable.

At this early stage, though, the only contact most of us have had with the end product is through books, magazines and ads on TV, and the occasional specimen you see out and about at weekends. Yes, it's odd. Before we get interested in babies, we never notice them. Even when we start looking, they're a bit thin on the ground. So where are they all?

But it doesn't matter. We think we know all the important stuff already. We know where the best people go to give birth; that we can get our figure back within days; that we can get a designer baby carrier; that we can buy it cashmere mittens; that playing Mozart will guarantee a genius. We know because we've done the research. We know we'll be the best parents ever. And the baby will be the best baby the world has ever seen. So let's get stuck in. After all, it's not fair to make the world wait any longer.

What we didn't factor in was the immensity of this particular project, and that those who had already beaten us in the egg and sperm race would be longing to tell us all about it.

'We'd decided to try for a baby and I was at the health food shop,' Lydia remembers. 'I'd just bought some pre-conceptual vitamins that looked pretty good, and I felt very pleased with myself, when this woman with a baby in one of those enormous three-wheeler buggies came in. I said hello to the baby and the woman seemed friendly. She looked at my vitamins and laughed knowingly. "I did a complete detox before I even started trying to get pregnant, and there are far better supplements than those – organic ones." I felt crushed but at the same time, I just wanted to get all the same stuff she'd got. So I wrote it all down feverishly. That was just the start of it.'

Suddenly it dawns on us just how high the bar has been set. If we're not right up there with an MA in Pregnancy, we've failed and failure is simply not an option. If we're not chanting pre-conceptual mantras, guzzling zinc (or whatever) and making our partners wear big baggy boxers for months before we even jettison the condoms, it's virtually child neglect. We get a nasty feeling in our stomachs – and it's not morning sickness – that we are being sucked into something. A bit like suspecting the person being so nice at the airport is a Scientologist. Our rational brain says, 'Hold it right there! I'm not falling for this.'

But we *do*.

Welcome to the madness of modern parenting.

The Thin Blue Line

Wham! Whether we managed to get pregnant straight away, or had to endure the living hell that is fertility treatment (ever been judged on the quality of your eggs before?), the realisation that we've created a new life brings a mixture of elation tinged with downright panic! Suddenly it feels as though the carpet has been pulled from under our feet. It's a new life all right – ours – and suddenly the old, predictable, under-control one starts to slip away.

If you're a bloke, there comes the validation that not only are you virile, you've joined the ranks of the grown-ups. And that makes you partnership material – the big swinging dick. But deep down, you're thinking, Help! Do I have to look as if I want to take six months' unpaid paternity leave? Or will that be as good as waving goodbye to promotion? How does the New Man get perceived at work – *truthfully now*? Damned if you do, damned if you don't.

If you're a woman, there comes the validation that you're fertile (phew!), but what the hell happens to *your* brilliant career now? The happy news can elicit the strangest response from those around you, especially at the office.

'When Dave announced at work that I was pregnant, everyone slapped him on the back,' says Carrie. 'When I announced it, people were nice but it was treated more like a problem. Was I going to be coming back straight after? What was I going to do about childcare? Would I go part-time? I could almost see the gleam in my colleagues' eyes as they thought about sharing out my clients between them.'

And to cap it all, your body no longer even feels like your own.

There you are – boobs like Dolly Parton's (but so sore, you can't bear your partner to touch them), constant puking, knackered all the time. And when you go to the antenatal clinic for the first time, you are sharing a waiting room with a load of tattooed teenagers. They must be in here for another reason surely. Then the midwife writes down on your notes that you're an 'elderly primagravida'! This was not what you signed up for!

Pregnancy is a great leveller all right.

Your New Club

At this stage parenting is terra nova, and we don't have a map, but there are compensations. We've become members of a new club without even having to apply, and our belly is our membership card. Our stamping ground becomes the previously unexplored maternity clothes and baby equipment shops. We had no idea there were so many retail opportunities, did we? Pregnancy, as a shopping experience, is hard to better, and spending shed loads of money is an excellent preparation for parenthood.

At last we've found the other parents, in the few shops they can get their enormous buggies into, and now we can set about observing them close up, and deciding what kind of parents *we're* going to be – in terms of style statement, that is.

For men, there's not too much choice in terms of role model. Obviously you're not going to go the Steve Bing/ Dwight Yorke route – cads that they are – but are you prepared to be as soppy as David Beckham or Jamie Oliver? You're dead proud too, of course, although not in a nasty macho way. But is it compulsory to have a tattoo? You're also completely terrified that you've lost your partner as you once knew her for ever, because she's acting so weird and moody, and the idea of natural birth scares you rigid, yet everyone's expecting you to be the strong one. How are you going to cope with all that? The same way other blokes do. By buying a huge great state-of-the-art buggy, of course. Suddenly Maclaren is the new McLaren.

Charles felt his Bugaboo definitely gave him
an edge, even with no baby inside.

'I've become obsessed with all the gear,' says James. 'I go up to couples in the street and ask them about their buggies. And the amazing thing is they all want to tell you about it, especially the blokes. Where once you'd be talking about the performance of your car, now all you can talk about is which buggy has the best handling. It's amazing how competitive it is to get the best.'

For pregnant women, there are all too many role models out there; trouble is, they're all uniformly gorgeous. Why, there's even a book called *The Yummy Mummy Handbook*. How nauseating is that? The reality for most of us, once our pregnancy starts to advance beyond the puking stage, is that we look and converse like a Teletubby, and that's on a good day. But we drag our knackered and ever increasing behinds to all those aqua natal classes, and slap on make-up to contrive that 'natural glow' we read about, but are still hoping for – because we're damned if anyone else is going to know how bloody hard we're finding it all. No point complaining about the competition any more – we're the competitors.

Buy the book

It's all so confusing, isn't it? Thank goodness for all the advice out there. Alarmingly, much of it is written by people who have only had one child and it's all so contradictory. But they're celebrities, so they must know what they're talking about.

Now every woman who has ever given birth could bore

for Britain about the details of her pregnancy and delivery. It's a brief spell when we're the centre of attention before being shunted aside by people wanting to gawp at the baby. You'll know, if you've been on the receiving end, just how dull it is, but if you let other couples bore you there's a chance they'll let you bore them in return.

If you're a celebrity, however, the normal rules don't apply. Everything they do is interesting – even when it's boring. This is why the list of celebrity pregnancy and parenting guides keeps getting longer and longer. They only have to have a bit part in *Holby City* and get up the duff. Suddenly they have a book deal, and now we can pay to be bored rigid by someone we've never even met. And, yes, they'll even tell us that pregnancy was a life-changing experience – like we didn't know that.

Cindy Crawford did it, Mel Giedroyc did it, Melanie Sykes, Libby Purves and Jools Oliver have all written books about motherhood. So, you may be asking yourself, what do they know? But if it's a choice between them and Gina Ford, you can begin to see the attraction.

Raising the perfect child

Have you noticed that, just when one theory of baby care becomes established, another one, saying completely the opposite, comes along? Perhaps all those experts get together and plan it that way, just to make sure they go on selling books? And why do we need to be told what to do by experts anyway? The very titles of their books are designed to make us anxious, so we need to buy the book to allay the fears they create. How about *Potty Training in One Week*? No pressure there.

'I can't prevent myself from buying these stupid books,' rants Louise. 'It's the titles. *The Contented Little Baby Book*, for goodness sake. Well, how can you say no to that? And *The Complete Secrets of Happy Children*. Not buying it seems irresponsible. And some of them even sound like management books, like *Seven Secrets of Successful Parents*. Or pet care manuals, like *The Baby Whisperer*. Bookshops are more of a threat to my health than unpasteurised Brie.'

Very public pregnancy

Pregnancy has never been so out there! Remember the Diana days when pregnant ladies disguised their condition behind tent-like dresses and coy euphemisms, and would disappear for a while, reappearing only when the yucky stuff was over, holding a swaddled and indistinct pudding. It was career death, of course, for working women and a woman never quite regained her pre-pregnancy glamour and sex appeal, moving immediately to the next generation up.

But that all changed in 1991, when famed celebrity photographer Annie Leibovitz photographed actress Demi Moore, naked and pregnant, for the cover of *Vanity Fair* magazine. This became one of the hottest selling issues in *Vanity Fair* history and a landmark of liberation for pregnant women everywhere. Liberation? Yeah, right. Only if you look like Demi. Semi Demi was no good at all.

Now it's open season for pregnant celebs. In terms of magazine circulation, the two very best sellers are celebrity pregnancy and celebrity drug rehab. And pregnancy has better photo opportunities. You can't open a glossy without coming nose to navel with the latest pregnosaur, from A-list downwards through the alphabet. They all seem to be at it and they're huge – at least in circulation terms – although rather less so in sheer physical terms. But more of that later.

In fact, pregnancy can be the making of a celebrity. And although it would be horribly cynical to imagine that parenting is part of a greater PR plan, there are plenty who owe their new-found high profile to the bun in the oven. Star mummies sell, both themselves and an idealised image of pregnancy and parenting. They look fantastic, they say they feel fantastic, they say they feel more fulfilled than ever before in their starry little lives. We flick the pages avidly, asking ourselves, does anyone actually believe this crap? Then find ourselves comparing our bovine form to Mrs Famous Bump's neat little silhouette. We know it's all hype, but doesn't it just get under your rapidly expanding skin?

Yummy pregnancy

In the late fifties, even Sylvia Plath, not known for her sunny outlook, wrote contentedly about being 'cow-heavy and floral' when she was pregnant. Today, the prevailing attitude towards the heavily pregnant body verges on disgust. So now we have to look sexy, gorgeous and available as well. It's enough to make your morning sickness last all day.

'It was the first time in years that I just ate what I felt like eating,' says Kate. 'It was incredibly liberating. But then I met this woman with a little neat bump, and lots of black Lycra (registered trade mark), and she kept going on about how she hadn't had to buy any maternity clothes. She was a whole month further on than me too. So, do you know what? I lied and said my baby was due before hers.'

Some of us react by taking weight control too far. A midwife says, 'I've known women go on diets *before* getting pregnant so they won't get too heavy by the end. The pregnancy and the delivery are all about them; it's almost like they've forgotten there's a baby involved. And I've seen them struggle to get into their pre-pregnancy jeans before they leave the hospital. The scariest thing is that some of them manage to!'

There is even a rumour that women have been asking for Caesarean sections to be scheduled as much as four weeks early, to avoid putting on that extra dollop of fat at the end of their pregnancy. Good to know they have their priorities straight. Which brings us on to . . .

Birth pangs

A survey carried out by *Mother & Baby* magazine found that three-quarters of new mothers they asked found childbirth 'more painful than they'd ever imagined'. Well, doh! Trying to expel a watermelon through your nose would probably be less daunting. And it's not as though we don't have time to think it over. Almost forty weeks, generally. And what goes up, must come down – usually the same route!

Once there was no option. You had your legs shoved into stirrups and pushed against gravity and the surgeon only went in if things got tricky. The problem for us now is the appearance of too much choice. What's on the menu? We can plump for scented candles, whale music and dimmed lights, or opt for three thirty on Tuesday afternoon in the operating theatre at a private hospital. Elective Caesareans are on the up and up – very much the celebrity choice – and the big advantage is that this high-tech route fits into the busy schedule and no loss of dignity. It's hard to see why anyone could imagine that recovering from major abdominal surgery and six weeks without being able to drive is somehow less inconvenient than the scenic route. Or maybe they're hoping to maintain their 'honeymoon freshness' – a repulsive expression that would make the most hardened want to gag.

Like all things these days the answer seems to be to throw money at it. We're so used to consumer choice these days that we apply it to the most unconsumer thing in the world. Most of us have Hobson's choice: NHS or NHS and though the whole creaking system tries to provide an amazing service, despite the best efforts of government, you've got to admit it's a time when a bit of luxury wouldn't go amiss. Actually, a clean loo with a door that locks would be a start.

Lucky for the Haves, these days, the only limit to their comfort at this trying time is the size of their bank balance. In London, the main private choices are the Portland Hospital, the Lindo Wing at St Mary's Hospital, the Hospital of St John and St Elizabeth (John and Lizzie's), and the Birth Centre. Each has its own philosophy and adherents.

'Posh labour has become like a holiday choice – you have the brochures,' says Sarah cynically. 'Will you go five star or barefoot luxury? You book yourself in at a time that suits you and pack your Louis Vuitton and away you go. Then you come back, fresh and relaxed, with your snaps and your little souvenir.'

The Portland attracts the likes of Liz Hurley, Posh and Zoë Ball, and is renowned for its luxury and excellent food – at a price. The Lindo hosted the royal deliveries of the Princess of Wales and Princess Michael of Kent. For the groovier boho set, anxious to start on earth-motherhood as they mean to go on , the Hospital of St John and St Elizabeth in north London, with its charismatic founder, Yehudi Gordon, emphasises über-natural childbirth: Jerry Hall, Heather Mills, Cate Blanchett, Elle McPherson and Kate Winslet, Sadie Frost and Emma Thompson pushed and grunted there. Birthing pools are standard and the luxury is of the laid-back variety. More democratic and distinctly low-tech, the Birth Centre in Tooting has tended to the needs of Davina McCall, Jane Horrocks, the late Paula Yates, Thandie Newton, Stella Tennant and Doon Mackichan. Hilariously, the Birth Centre justifies its fees by comparison with other purchases, including school fees, sofas, mortgage payments, two weeks in Barbados and weddings.

'I have two friends who gave birth in completely different ways,' Sarah continues. 'One high-tech and the other natural, and each is convinced her way is the *only* way to go. They corner me on their own and bang on about the pros and cons, trying to recruit me to their gang! It's a bit like being back in the playground. And their babies both look and smell the same to me.'

Still not sure what you want? You could always follow Madonna's example and flee the country altogether. What about France, you hear yourself thinking, because you read somewhere they give you a glass of wine after the birth. Beats NHS tea any day.

Sadly, there is no definitive research about the effect different birthing methods have on the children the babies become. Are Zen-born ones really calmer than those ripped untimely? When he's screaming blue murder in the supermarket queue, it all seems wonderfully irrelevant.

Telling tales

Whatever happens during the delivery, we have to commit it all to memory, because we will dine out on it for the next few years and, like the Ancient Mariner, we find ourselves stopping people and relating our gory tale whether they want to hear it or not. What! Only one in three? The other two got off lightly.

This cringe-making frankness astonishes our mothers who were so coy about their own experiences they failed entirely to mention that they had you in under two hours.

Now you know why you had Millie in the hospital car park. Or that they laboured for thirty-six hours. You'd have gone for a section straight away if you'd known.

If you've already started swapping stories on the circuit, you'll already know that the best-in-show rosette will always be reserved for the women who struggled through hours of agonising labour, fully conscious and unaided, bravely turning away pethidine and sticking remorselessly to their birth plan. If you had an elective section, you might as well give up and go home. No one wants to hear about it. You loser.

Delivery Dads

Only a generation ago, the only active role a man had in the birth of his child was to pace up and down and hand out the cigars once everything was done and dusted. Now 90 per cent of dads are present – and there's a lot of pressure for them to be there. How on earth did that happen? And did anyone think to ask if that's what anyone wanted?

In the 1960s, one father-to-be in Chicago had to hand-cuff himself to his partner's trolley so he could not be removed from the delivery suite! One similarly eager dad, more recently, had been to all the classes and read all the books, but it didn't prepare him for what happened. 'I was all ready,' he whines, 'with ice chips in a flask and tennis balls in a sock to massage Lydia's back. She turned into a complete harpy, and screamed at me to "**** off" with my ice chips. And she squeezed my hand so hard, it took weeks for the sensation to come back properly.'

Nowadays, fathers are more likely to have to chain themselves to the vending machine if they don't want to be part of the birth. It takes a brave man to come right out and say he doesn't want to be there. One of the few who've done so is the chef Gordon Ramsay, no stranger to stressful situations, who admitted that he did not attend any of his four children's births. Funny. They're all so keen to be there for conception.

Nick, a father of four, says: 'I managed to avoid being at the birth with the first three. The first time I was at work. With the next two, being quite close together, I had to look after the older ones. With the last one, though, I'd run out of excuses. I tried everything. Going out to make phone calls, offering to go home and check on things, going to the loo. I really thought I was going to faint. I stayed well away from the business end, I can tell you.'

But nowadays daddy is expected to be in the delivery room witnessing every stage of baby's arrival – even if it is a Caesarean. 'An operating theatre, seeing his wife having major abdominal surgery, is not the right place for a man to be,' says a seasoned obstetrician. 'It's hard for medical students first time and they're not even emotionally involved. The best place for a man to be during a Caesarean is somewhere else.'

Instead there they are with the camcorder, getting in everyone's way, recording every pant and grunt. The end result you subject your friends to is somewhere between *Alien* and a soft porn flick. *Emmanuelle Bears Down*?

Get Real

Thirty years ago, no one expected very much of women when they had delivered. They could spend three weeks in their dressing gown and learn the scary lessons of new motherhood in the privacy of their own home, with the help of their mum or a starched maternity nurse.

Now you are expected to have pinged back into shape just like Liz Hurley, and to be a dab hand at changing nappies straight away. It's like suddenly being asked to fly a jumbo jet without the training. And it's a conspiracy of silence! Why won't somebody break rank and just say how bloody hard it is? Let's face it, most of us have still not regained our shape twenty-two months after giving birth and some of us will still be waiting for it to happen after twenty-two years. Yet apparently 97 per cent of us feel 'unhappy about our bodies after having a baby'.

So if everyone else is as fat and blobby as we are, why are we so bothered about it? It's the elastic celebs that are the freaks, not us.

And then there's the baby to contend with. 'Motherhood hit me like an oncoming train,' admits Polly. 'I had absolutely no idea what was coming. Nothing in my education has prepared me for it. Why couldn't I get him to sleep? How hard could it be? I've got an MBA, for God's sake.'

Bloody hard – that's how hard – and it's no easier for the over-educated. This is when the panic sets in. Everyone else seems to be finding it so easy, don't they? The happy truth is they're not, actually. Everyone's finding it as tough as you are but, like admitting to being hopeless in bed, it's the hardest thing to confess to.

You have this sneaky feeling that because you brought it on yourself, you have to grin and bear it, and it's ten times worse if you struggled to get there in the first place.

'We did IVF eight times,' says Gail. 'How could I admit to being less than ecstatic 24/7 when the whole process had taken years and cost us about as much as a family car!'

It's like your mother used to say when the stilettos you'd insisted on started to pinch: you've only yourself to blame. You're damned if you'll admit it, and if everyone else seems to find it easy you'd better pretend you do too. It's no wonder we flounder.

Tizzie Hall, an Australian sleep guru, says we are the most inexperienced mothers in history. 'We don't grow up with small siblings to practise on, we don't see babies around us. Often the first baby we ever hold is our own. And we live far from our families so have little support or advice.' She may be talking about the thousands of miles between Sydney and Perth, but when you have a colicky newborn, Sydenham to your mother in Purley can seem light years away.

Jenny remembers, 'Everyone said, "Follow your instincts, follow your instincts, your instincts will take over." And it just didn't make any sense to me. The only instinct I had was to run away.'

Fran winces at the memory: 'Oh! Those early days of motherhood; being left with a tiny baby and wanting to yell to my husband's departing back, as he headed off to work and the sanity of the adult world, "Please don't leave me, what am I supposed to do?" So I tried to build structure in the day. I would go to various drop-ins and spent a great deal of my time at the clinic having Harvey weighed. It became a pretty full-time occupation.'

Most of us cope, just, but, out of our skulls on hormones and fatigue, it's usually all we can do to find ourselves a clean pair of knickers. Where did the chick in the snappy suit and the briefcase go?

She's out there all right. She's that Super-Mum. The one who's chairing a meeting forty-eight hours after delivery. The one who's in full slap when you haven't had time to wash your hair for three weeks. The one who's making you feel totally inadequate as you lumber with your pram. Rest assured it's nothing compared to the pressure she's putting on herself.

'When I see women for their six-week check,' says a GP, 'the ones I don't worry about are the ones with their sweatshirts on inside out, who tell me they haven't slept since the birth and they feel like a blob. That's perfectly normal. It's the ones who've put on make-up and have ironed their co-ordinated outfits and say everything is fantastic that worry me. They're the ones trying to live up to unrealistic standards.'

Post-natal depression? Moi?

Tits Up

Breast is best! Breast is best! (So anything else is complete pants.) That may not be exactly what they say, but we all know that's what they mean. Okay, it may be natural, but it's far from simple. Breastfeeding has gone on for as long as women have had boobs, but we make it horribly tricky for ourselves these days, trying to fit it in with our busy, busy lives.

'There was this really thick girl in hospital, right across from me,' says Amanda, a merchant banker. 'A real pramface. And she was managing it no bother – baby latching on, good supply, the lot. And the way she looked over at me, so smug. Well, to be quite honest, it was probably the way I'd have looked at her in any other context in the world. I was really floundering and I bet the midwives were thinking, Bloody career women. And, just for the record, let me say there's nothing more stressful than being told to relax all the bloody time.'

And even if you do manage to get feeding going, the advice is still completely contradictory. But what's a girl to do? You've got Gina Ford telling you to feed to a schedule, you've got another batch of experts telling you to feed on demand. If you feed to schedule, there's a good chance your supply of milk will decrease. If you feed on demand, you'll never get a routine established. So which is it?

'I can't believe what's happened to me. I used to be able to do things,' says Jane. 'And I'm sitting here, advice book in hand, on the phone to my breastfeeding counsellor, with cabbage leaves down my bra, tits like boulders and a screaming baby.'

Lucy gave up trying, but still felt the pressure. 'I did go to my after-birth yoga class with the baby and lied about it and said I was breastfeeding. And the baby's not even a week old!'

These days breastfeeding is the Battle of the Boobs. 'I became obsessed with other women's tits,' says Helen. 'If I saw a woman with a baby and enormous knockers I'd want to stab her!' And the self-satisfaction of those who can!

'I was sitting at a post-natal get-together of my NCT group – I still think of them as ordeal by home-made flapjack – and Tom was fractious,' says Verity. 'He just wouldn't feed and I knew it was because I was tired and production was low. One of the other mothers looked over at me sympathetically, baby to her breast, and asked, sweetly, if I'd like to use some milk from the fridge she'd expressed earlier! I never went back.'

Of course all good cows are judged by their milk production quotas, but what is it that makes people who were once our friends – intelligent, sensitive women – suddenly lose all modesty and brag about their skills at lactation?

Dawn is amazed by it all: 'I was sitting recently with a group of woman having coffee,' she says. 'One admitted she was struggling with breastfeeding and worrying about having enough milk, then this insensitive cow – careful choice of word there – pipes up with, "Oh, God, when I was breastfeeding I just had SO much of it, I couldn't get it to stop. I'd lie in the bath and there'd be, you know, a layer of cream forming around me. It was amazing!" Horrified silence all round . . .'

If you did manage it and it's all systems go, then good on ya, Daisy. The World Health Organisation loves you. The NCT loves you. Every childbirth and parenting pundit loves you. But enough of this love fest. If breast-feeding is good, why are we still finding ourselves squatting in bathrooms trying to nurse, fumbling with shawls, apologising all the time, being asked to leave restaurants and coffee houses, and treated like social pariahs? You'd think, wouldn't you, that in these liberated times you could get your boobs out without being vilified for it?

At least if our mothers did it (which few of them did – it interrupted cocktail parties) they did it in the privacy of their own home, with a fag and a G&T to while away the boredom. Our problem, silly us, is that we still want to make like single girls and meet girlfriends for coffee. Tits and caramel macchiato don't mix.

Naming or shaming?

Choosing a name for the baby ought to be the fun bit – especially when we, as a generation, have such boring names. We were all called Katherine or James. A bit of creativity in the naming department is the reward for necking all those vitamins, going to all those NCT classes and hospital appointments. It's the only thing in the uncertain world of birth and labour that you really do have control over, so there's all the more pressure to get it right. Is a single word capable of telling the world just how utterly perfect your child is going to be?

Naturally the celebs take the Oscars for absurdity here. Gwyneth's Apple and Moses, Helen Hunt's MaKena Lei, Cate Blanchett's Roman, Heidi Klum's Leni, Courteney Cox Arquette's Coco: they sound like Chihuahuas, poor little sods. But they are not the only ones who completely lose the plot when they name their babies. Quite a lot of parents seem to have this shameless urge to be original and unique. To make their babies into a limited edition. Exclusive.

But with all the weird and wacky names around, why is it getting harder and harder to choose something? It is a sign of the times that a new book, *Cool Names for Babies*, by Pamela Redmond Satran and Linda Rosenkrantz, has recently been published. All this competition has given rise to a terrifying new trend, 'Name Rage'.

'We spent ages coming up with the name for our baby,' says Mary. 'And my stupid husband went and confided in a friend. Soon after that a friend of the friend got in first and used *our* name for *their* baby. I was livid. We never speak to them now.'

'I called my daughter Nutmeg,' opined one old hippy, 'because I felt it would help her to build her character.' Well, let's hope she builds enough to turn round and give her parents a sharp slap when she is tall enough.

Why, oh why don't they save up the wacky ideas for middle names? Or, better still, get themselves a cat.

However, the ramifications of getting the name wrong are terrifying if recent research is to be believed. Psychiatrists have found that men named Wayne were more likely to be considered malingering, feigning and personality-disordered in diagnosis than those called Matthew. So that cuts down the choices a bit. The study concluded that doctors may stereotype patients on the basis of their names. What would they make of Tiger Lily and Dweezil?

Sleep – please?

It is a universal truth that a baby is a nocturnal creature, sleeping adorably during the day and yelling blue murder from 9 p.m. onwards, making any attempt at civilised meals or conversation between parents utterly impossible. After being passed from parent to exhausted parent for a few hours, the baby will sleep intermittently from about 11 p.m. until 2 a.m., when it will wake again and require constant feeding to nourish it for a hard day of sleeping from about 9 a.m.

Terrible sleepers are probably nothing new. Mothers throughout history have paced the nursery floor singing lullabies, but that was all very well in the days when they had all day to sleep with them. Or nannies to do the pacing. But when you have just got home from a sales conference, or have two other children to consider, it's living torture.

Our mistake is that we are guilty of *trying to get back to normal as soon as possible*, of kidding ourselves it won't be like that for us, so we ignore the voices of warning.

Instead we run around like headless chickens at 3 a.m. trying to find solutions. John admits, 'We tried everything: swaddling, black-out curtains, white noise, formula top-ups. Most of the things we tried did work – once – and we'd think we were on to something. But the next night, we'd be back to square one. One night, at about 3 a.m., we even moved the cot so it was lying north–south rather than east–west. Then it was magnetic mattresses. Anything!'

The next mistake we make is to believe that other people's babies are always sleeping more than our own – it's a ripe area for one-upmanship and since you're not there at midnight to check, the big fat liars can get away with it. At least some of them 'fessed up in another survey by *Mother & Baby* magazine, which found that during the first four months, mothers average fewer than four hours' sleep a night. Sometimes the media can be our friend!

And, naturally, where there is a problem, there'll be someone out there prepared to tell you you're doing it all wrong. Thanks again, Gina! But wouldn't you pay anything to make the baby sleep through? Now you can hire a night-time nanny to solve the problem for you. In just two nights, they claim to be able to get your baby into good sleep habits. Basically, you pay them to leave your baby to cry. How crazy is that?

'My partner actually had to restrain me to stop me going to Tim when we decided to try controlled crying,' says a quivering Tracey. 'I think I was crying more than the baby by the end of it, and even though in my heart I knew I didn't agree with the advice in the baby manual, I went along with it like a lemming.'

But fear not, Tracey. A scientist has come to your rescue. A study has shown that the best way to ensure your child grows up as a 'calm, healthy adult' is to let him sleep in your bed *until he is five*. Never mind that you will get no sleep from his wriggling, you'll have offspring with good chi and there'll always be plenty of room in the bed because your partner will have buggered off in despair ages ago.

'We've got to get to lunch on time. I don't
want them to twig she isn't sleeping through.'

Mama wars

With all the world today in strife, you might think we would cut each other some slack. That motherhood, the great leveller, would serve as a safe house where civility and mutual respect prevail. If only. Working mothers and stay-at-home mothers have been staging a vicious, guerrilla war against each other since the Equal Opportunities Commission first opened its doors.

Jackie says, 'There's nothing yummy about being a stay-at-home mummy. I love Ella to pieces, but it's the hardest work I've ever done and it's more than full-time. I get so pissed off with people asking what I do and then looking over my shoulder to see if there's someone more interesting when I say I'm a full-time mother. They make me feel as though I've taken the cop-out route.'

Celine sees it from the other side: 'My partner is a composer and he works from home. I'm a teacher and I can't work from home. What could be more logical than for me to go out and him to stay with Charlotte. But you'd think I was Cruella DeVil the way some of the stay-at-home mums treat me. And when he takes Charlotte out shopping, just because he's a bloke, he gets all these women helping him! Meanwhile I'm racked with guilt.'

Alex is more direct: 'I'm doing the job I spent years training for. Why should I feel guilty about that?'

Then there's Rachel: 'I'm fed up of being the only mother at mother and baby groups. Most of the other women there are nannies and they won't talk to me.'

It seems we can't do right for doing wrong! So much

expected, so little help and society so ready to blame. We decide to climb off the career ladder and we are a parasite. We decide to stay on it, and we are a bad, bad woman. The legislation is pretty much in place to allow parents to return to work, if we want or need to, yet we still feel like second-class citizens.

Men can't win either. One (male) business director admits: 'I wouldn't let on to doing the school run or wanting to be at one of my kids' events because it might affect how my peer group perceives me. I opened my briefcase in a meeting the other day and there was a copy of *Little Red Train* in there. I slammed it shut quickly before anyone noticed as if it was a dirty magazine!'

'If I was in a pinch, I'd only turn to another working mother,' confides Sally, an estate agent and the mother of two young boys. 'Even my closest friends lord it over me. One really close girlfriend sighed deeply when I asked her to collect Dan from swimming for me because I'd been held up with a viewing. "Oh, you career girls," she said. "Always putting work first!" I could have slapped her!'

Of course the working mum will get her own back when the children have flown the nest and the stay-at-homer decides to embark on the tricky route of career rebirth. But then she did give her children the best years.

Life after birth: it's a social life, Jim, but not as we know it

Remember that moment in *Sex and the City* when Miranda, new mother in denial, tries to rejoin the normal world and takes her baby out to a restaurant with her

mates. 'Nothing has to change. Just thi...
purse.' The big purse promptly vomits.

So is it possible to combine a baby wi...
these days? Well, no. Not really. Child-free fi...
come to the conclusion that we're part of an ....al
cult, trying to recruit new members to parent.ood. We,
meanwhile, have to construct a new life for ourselves
among the Parent People, who know Milton isn't neces-
sarily a poet and where we can talk about our piles and
stitches with complete strangers, and nobody looks at us
funny.

Outside that safe and lovely place, there's the awful
realisation that we have become social pariahs.

'I have to confess that these days I try and avoid my
friends with babies,' says Caroline, unreassuringly.
'They are so boring, with their endless chat about
nappies and their contents. They can never come out
and when they do they keep yawning, spend the whole
time looking at their watches then worry about their
boobs leaking.'

Then that huge car we bought is too big to park. We
can't take that lovely big buggy into any of the shops we
want to go to because it won't fit through the doors. We
can't live the life we did before because no restaurant
really wants us there. There's nowhere to change the baby
that's quite clean enough and nowhere we feel comfortable breastfeeding. Parks are full of huge menacing two-
year-olds and, frankly, with all the clobber we were talked
into, by the time we're ready to leave the house, it's time
to come home again.

ιow we know why we never really saw anyone with a ιaby out and about, in those far-off days of our pregnancy. They were all at home fretting, just like we are now, or at each other's houses, pretending to each other that their baby sleeps through.

The Top Ten Most Oppressive Book Titles Ever

The Seven Sins of Parenting an Only Child

The Baby Whisperer Solves All Your Problems

Brain Child: How Smart Parents Make Smart Kids

The Yummy Mummy's Survival Guide

Potty Training in Less Than a Day

Creating Kids Who Can Concentrate

Body After Baby: The Simple 30 Day Plan to Lose Your Baby
   Weight

Optimum Nutrition for Your Child's Mind

The Science of Parenting: Practical Guidance on Sleep,
   Crying, Play and Building Emotional Wellbeing for Life

365 Creative Days of Play

From Kid to Superkid

The Top Ten Silliest Childcare Book Titles Ever

125 Brain Games for Babies

Sippy Cups are Not for Chardonnay

101 Educational Conversations with Your Kindergartner-1st
   Grader

Fresh Milk: The Secret Life of Breasts

The Three Martini Playdate

Baby Signing (Publisher? Amazing Baby)

O'Baby: The Irish Baby Name Book

Laughin'fertility: A Bundle of Observations for the Baby-
Making Challenged (Wince-making awful!)
Baby-gami: Baby Wrapping for Beginners
Fathers' Liberation Ethics: Holistic Ethical Advocacy for Active
Nurturant Fathering (Zzzzz . . .)

Wisdom before the Event
(or things you wish you'd never said)

I'm going to give birth without pain relief
I won't talk about the baby all the time
I won't be one of those women/men who bore other people
senseless
I'll breastfeed of course
I'd never use a dummy
Our baby will never sleep in our bed
I'd never smack my children!
I'll never bribe them with sweets
Having a baby will not change my life

3
Trial By Party Bag

Jelly and ice cream, jelly and ice cream. Oh, it used to be so simple then. Uncle George with his ukulele, a couple of rounds of Pass the Parcel and Pin the Tail on the Donkey, then settle down for a tea of bread and butter (which you had to eat first before you were allowed the party ring biscuits). The iced gems were always left on the plate because they were and still are disgusting. Then you'd run around the garden in your short white socks, knowing your mother would tear you off a strip for getting them covered in grass stains, until home time at half past five when you'd be handed a slice of the *home-made* cake wrapped in a paper napkin and, if you were lucky, a balloon, which would burst in the back of the car – though that was a good thing because it was obscuring your mother's view out of the back window anyway.

Your feet would hurt from the elastic on your blue patent party shoes, and your dress would have ripped when someone had stood on the sash when you were on the space hopper, but Uncle George had been funny – even though you'd seen the rabbit-out-of-the-hat gag six times before – and you had a trip to see *Bedknobs and Broomsticks* with Gillian from 3B after half-term to look forward to, because her mum had booked it at the Odeon as her special birthday treat.

We didn't seem to have parties every year then, except for my friend Tracy who was quite rich and spoilt and a select group of us used to go to the leisure centre with her to swim. Our brothers had football parties, refereed by unfit fathers who would give away penalties unfairly and precipitate tears and time out in your bedroom 'until you have calmed down'. There might have been war games which involved hiding with water pistols behind trees or Kick the Can, which was scary if you were 'it', and the boys would go to any lengths, even resorting to violence, to get to the can before you.

So we progressed through the party years. Games got more and more daring – Blockey 1-2-3 in the dark with torches? – until we hit our teens and exploded in a burst of hormones. Instead of flicking ice cream at smelly George Dickson and playing Blind Man's Buff with him, you'd be pinned against the wall of the village hall trying to flick flirtatious looks at a now much taller (and strangely attractive) George Dickson and thinking about doing other things in the buff with him. We'd have hot dogs and fruit punch and shuffle to 10CC *I'm Not In Love*, while being held in the sweaty grip of a boy who wasn't George Dickson, until someone put the lights back on because it was eleven thirty and Dad had arrived to collect you in the Ford Sierra.

Your own party would have passed in a haze of excitement and a vague feeling of nausea brought on by too much dandelion and burdock, and the hope that everyone would leave very soon so you could open that tantalising pile of presents, which would include a 6-inch single of 'Crazy Horses' by the Osmonds, a pink troll and a furry orange pencil case.

That was then . . .

Of course our birthdays used to come around slower when we were younger, but have you noticed how our own children's birthdays seem to arrive about a month after last year's? Or at least that's when you start planning the next one.

'What happened to the big celebration?' asks Gemma. 'When once only Big Birthdays, like the eighteenth and twenty-first, warranted Big Plans, now all birthdays seem to involve advance planning on the scale of a task force. We know people who I can't help thinking have peaked a bit soon with a tenth birthday bash. What will they do for an encore?'

Frankly, a party for a hundred adults is preferable to a shindig for twenty or thirty (or actually any number of) children. Children are now so unstinting in their judgements, with absolutely no grasp of the social graces whereby you pretend you are having a good time even if it's dire and you'd rather be anywhere else on earth. But don't you sense that this feeling of being judged is now heightened to such intense levels thanks to the weight of expectation?

And that is the crux of the Birthday Party Angst that has us all in its grip: *expectation*. No longer will simple, brief and easy suffice. In fact their first birthday, when they are more interested in the paper and the cardboard box, is the one and only time when we seem to be able to get away with anything. Trouble is no one told us at the time!

But added to expectation – and we have to be big and brave to admit this – isn't it just possible that a birthday party is our once-a-year chance (and more if you have several kids) to invite all our friends and other parents in, and show them just what marvellous parents we are?

'Yup, that's me!' says Freya sheepishly. 'I hold my hands up and admit that I get a bit of a kick when other parents say, "Wow!" I mean, you've got to make sure they know how much effort you've put in, don't you? How else would they know?'

The Honeymoon Period: Ages 1–3

To be really prepared these days, you have to start thinking about birthday parties at about the point at which the child is to be conceived. Saddle yourself with a January baby and the options for parties are severely restricted as it gets older. 'Weather permitting' are words that strike fear into any party organiser's soul. Don't know about you, but not many people would dare risk a slaved-over Pirates Extravaganza being rained off and then be lumbered with thirty expectant faces turned to you for entertainment. No, really the only time we should be thinking about risking pregnancy is between August and December (though even that might be leaving it a bit late).

At least these early years are the simple ones when birthday parties are a genuine celebration of the miracle of our children. Most one-year-olds are pretty clueless about the birthday concept anyway, but know to smile benignly when a helium balloon is waved at them because it means lots of lovely attention. One friend does admit to staying up late the night before to ice out Happy 1st Birthday on the top of a chocolate cake, vaguely aware of the absurdity of what she was doing. Could the fact that her mother-in-law was coming over for tea the next day have had anything to do with it?

At least at this early stage you don't have to contend with the 'invite the whole class' dilemma and can only hope that the other mothers there will be as obsessed as you are with potty training so will fail to notice any shortcomings on your part – though, as with any gathering of other parents, that in itself brings on its own stresses! The Helicopter Mother will be around the table like a persistent bluebottle of course.

'It's feeble I know but I found myself apologising all the time!' Alison rants. 'I found myself justifying everything and saying weakly, "Oh, do you think so," when one Heli mum pointed out earnestly how bread sticks can be awfully sharp on their little mouths.'

The trouble is that, with a fairly poor level of conversational subject matter among the partygoers, you are left to converse with the other parents, who you hardly know but met at toddler group. They can't leave their offspring with you (thank God!), but the only thing you have in common with them is that you have children the same age, which makes you cling together like survivors in a shipwreck. No one will admit they are knackered but will tell you how many teeth their darling has and laugh, saying, 'Never mind, you don't see many adults with only four,' when you admit that your child has only popped the top and bottom two.

This is the only time in their lives that children seem to be unaffected by peer or commercial pressure. They think the adverts on ITV are part of the programme so won't be too judgemental about the level of the bash or the quality of the present. But it's not really about them, is it? It takes courage to buck the trend and get away with 'Come round for tea and a bit of cake'. But this party business is uncharted territory, isn't it? We can have friends round for dinner, and probably arranged our own weddings, but a Children's Party? Now that's a whole new challenge.

'I didn't sleep for two nights.' Beth laughs. 'And when the first child arrived, I broke into a muck sweat. I opened a bottle of wine and by the time the parents came to collect them, I was half cut!'

'Oh, God! I was so terrified that I ended up being horrible to my son – and it was his party!' wails Harriet. 'He ended up in tears and so did I!'

But we needn't worry if we are nervous about how we should handle the stress – there's plenty of advice out there in books and websites. Don't have the party at nap time; don't have balloons that may burst and startle children; offer carrot sticks and hummus or guacamole, for goodness sake; sweeten your cake with apple juice not sugar; don't offer chocolate . . .

'Talk to your toddler about what they would like for their party a few weeks before the event,' suggests one child guru. Come on! There are times when you can take inclusion too far. Don't they know toddlers have absolutely no idea of timescales and will think you mean tomorrow? Though of course you find yourself asking the little chap anyway because you don't want him to feel excluded. You are even given – and probably heed – advice on how to word the actual invitation. One supplier advertises ready done invitations with the words 'first impressions count'. What is this – a party invite or a job application?

The Tween Years: piling on the pressure

From four onwards, though, it's party-time *extraordinaire* when there is about one party a week at least and the pressure is more full-on than an A-list celeb's diary. School has started and with it a whole new seam of children and their parties and the ensuing party neurosis. You come home from collecting your child from a class-mate's Karate Party and think, How the hell will I top that? And implicit in the rave reviews your child gives of it is, How the hell will you top that? Or at least you read it that way.

A recent report by Virgin Credit Card reveals that over half of UK parents are suffering from 'Posh Party Syndrome', and we fork out over £1.25 billion a year on our kids' birthday parties. Not each one of us of course, though it may feel like it. That's an average of £181.50

per party – and if that's the average a scary number of us must be spending a lot more. In London it's about £221 per party, which means if you invited fifteen children that would be nearly £15 a head – probably more than the value of the gift they bring with them – and that's before you've bought a present for *your* child. According to another report, it's the fifth birthday that is the biggy with over half of 3,500 parents polled saying they'd spend over £500 on it. Based on population numbers, that's about £128 million being spent on children turning five this year alone!

These reports are done by banks and credit card companies – as well they might be as you'll have to remortgage to afford it – but the most alarming finding is this: over half of UK parents admit that they feel under pressure to compete with other parents. Oh, crikey, so that's it: we've been rumbled. It's not about giving our children the very best. It's not about imitating celebrity parties because your child is every bit as special as Brooklyn or Romeo Beckham. It's about what the *other parents think*. Another report – if you can believe companies carry out these things – states eight out of ten parents said that other parents are always trying to show off by throwing the biggest and best birthday bash. That's either sociological observation on the part of the respondents, or paranoia.

One party organiser we spoke to confirms it all. 'Parents get very nervous about parties,' she said. 'They want their children to look good in front of their friends and they want to look good in front of their friends. We always prepare tea and coffee for the parents who are staying at our parties and, at one party as people arrived, the hostess, ignoring the children, was running over to ask them what they wanted to drink. It was as if they might think she had failed in some way if she didn't ensure they had what they wanted.'

Another party organiser is more blunt: 'It is all about impressing other people.'

The bar is set pretty high, so what do we find ourselves doing? Like getting an interior decorator in to choose our curtains, we get in a professional to do our kids' parties, and what they offer now is a million miles from pinning the tail on the donkey. Perhaps in our agonisingly self-conscious desire to avoid anyone losing – how would they cope with the failure? – we studiously avoid competitive games and plump for pamper or makeover parties (from age six) where, in some sort of paedophiliac fantasy, little girls can all look beautiful as they have their nails painted and their hair done in any from a 'range of 14 styles' while they sip little cocktails and look like something from the Elizabeth Arden salon in the 1950s. Yippee! They can round it all off with 'some body art tattoos applied to finish your transformation to Pamper Princess, Disco Diva, or Teenage Belle' before – and here's the critical bit – 'being collected by shocked and *impressed* parents' as it says on one piece of sales literature. (Apoplectic more like.) Another one sounds so insincere we're not even sure they aren't being sarcastic: 'From 5 to 9 years – give your little darling's [sic] a birthday to remember'.

On the assumption that not many twelve-year-old boys

would go for beauty parties, we call in the SAS of party planners to exploit the testosterone rush with quad bike parties and paint balling at upwards of £200. But we fall for the set price, little realising that an impassioned adolescent can discharge 200 paint balls in no time and then come begging for seven quid to get a few more. Two hours later and we are writing a cheque to the organisers for £350. Yes, dear reader, that sucker was me.

'We did go karting,' whispers Penny (surname withheld), 'and I paid for half with a cheque and the rest with cash so my husband wouldn't know how much it had cost.' Marital deception? Things are getting out of hand.

Parties have taken on the same dimensions as corporate events. You find yourself going the whole hog. He wants action? You find yourself hiring a tank and Parachute Regiment lookalikes in combats. She wants a bouncy castle? Why stop there? Hire a fairground to come to your house. Yes, really, it's been done.

Party goods and party planning is a massive industry, though Peter Robertson of Twizzle, the society party planners with whom some parents spend over £10,000 a party, reckons it's not in response to parents wanting to get one up on the Joneses. It's hard not to think he's being a bit too charitable or concerned his customers might be listening. 'We do parties for busy working mums, often successful business women,' he says, 'who simply don't have the time. It's more than just trying to impress.' Though he did admit a look of satisfaction on the faces of the hosts as they smiled modestly at the gasps of admiration from collecting parents.

As if to compound the pressure, at the end of the credit card birthday spending report, published on the web, were links to websites with suggestions for themes and party games. Even as you look at them you can feel the pressure building. It isn't: 'Gosh that's a good idea. I'll keep that in mind.' It's: 'Hell, I've never done that. Should I have had a Piñata? And what is one anyway? Yoga parties – what?'

The wealth of information, advice, ideas, goodies to buy for this age group is frankly overwhelming, but it's the wording that is most alarming: 'We recognise the importance of a fantastic going home present . . .' or 'this theme is always a success'. It's meant to help, but all it does is heap on the pressure. If you don't heed the advice, is the underlying message, you might *fail*.

You may not approve but you daren't break ranks. So it is a certain madness descends: what happened to your sense of proportion? There you are at midnight, propped up by a glass of Glenmorangie, wrapping up a *Now That's What I Call Music* CD (you can please all of the people all of the time) inside layer upon layer of paper for Pass the Parcel, remembering of course to insert a little something between each layer so *no one loses out*. This is what writer Lesley Thomas calls: 'part of a new and rather cowardly style of parenting in which Mummy and Daddy never want to be the bad guy'. She goes on: 'I don't think it's kind to shield children from the lesson that "you win some, you lose some".'

Then there's the party bag. The thing that says as much about us as the car we drive. The yardstick of the success of our party, and therefore us as parents, is the contents of the party bag. So you find yourself stuffing water pistols and Top Trumps into a cheap but jolly plastic bag, racked with uncertainty: too much? too little? If it's not up to standard, will your child be invited to the next party? Yet you know deep down (and resentfully) that it will all be discarded and put in the bin anyway when they get home.

And then what you thought was okay seems so mean and tacky when you hear that at Georgie's party they got a little book as a going-home present, with a mini Mars Bar attached as a special treat. Okay, so Georgie's mum is in publishing and she is a good friend of yours, but somehow you feel a bit let down. She's played dirty and used her position to get one over on everyone. In the words of Dolly Parton: please don't do it just because you can.

You snarl for a bit and feel stupid until you and Georgie's mum can both laugh together when you hear about the total absurdity of the dinner dance, with linen tablecloths, black tie and 'champagne' reception with sparkling apple juice, for a five-year-old. Really.

Going solo

Of course party success (and, ergo, parent success) is measured in quite the opposite way too: by being the parent who *did it all herself* . . . We do this one of two ways: we hire not one, not two but five bouncy castles of different shapes and have an activity party, or we get all creative and have princes and princesses parties. 'I spent hours trawling places like Currys and stuffing giant-sized old washing machine boxes into the back of my car,' says

Jennifer. 'Then it took ages to make castles out of them. The children made their own crowns out of crafty bits I'd laid out on a table and they proceeded to wreck the boxes.' And how did she feel for her efforts? Just a teensy bit pleased with herself? 'Well, yes, I suppose I did feel a certain amount of satisfaction when the leisure-centre-party mothers came to collect their offspring and oohed and aahed in admiration.'

Of course the trickiest issue is The Cake. Naturally we all know that it will be cut, wrapped in a napkin, popped in the party bag and binned. So what do you do? Slave over it for hours, creating something that looks a bit like Hogwarts out of Royal icing, or do you nip into the supermarket for a ready made, iced, utterly disgusting version based around some TV theme? It's a tough call.

'I can do the hired-in entertainer,' says Helen, 'but I just can't bring myself to buy a birthday cake. I have to make it – it's a matter of principle – and the one and only time I did cave in and buy one the entertainer asked my daughter if Mummy had made it.'

Marie takes the whole cake-making issue so seriously she makes one for the candle-blowing-out ceremony, but it's such a work of art she won't actually let the children eat it. In fact no one eats it. It is simply photographed for the album and is left out to be admired until too stale to eat. Nope, she buys one in to cut up for the party bag.

Take that route though and there is always the danger a guest's mother will eat it from the napkin in the party bag; then what might she think?!

Upping the ante

Phew, as they get a bit older you heave a sigh of relief because you no longer have to fret about trial by Victoria sponge, nor do you have to invite the whole class. At last we can slough off that irritating whingey little child whose mother always hung around in case he proved to be allergic to the type of bread we were using for the sandwiches. She needn't have worried, they went un-touched anyway, along with the hummus, but we had to provide them, didn't we? What we do have to do now, though, is seriously *impress*. Parties for anything over the age of eleven have to be very cool indeed and we end up feeling even more image-conscious than our coy, excru-ciatingly embarrassed pre-pubescent child.

A trip to the skating rink or the leisure centre just won't wash. Bowling? Too quick, too noisy – and the shoe-sharing? Yeuch. Laser Quest? Too last year. So you end up booking one of those wind-tunnel sky-diving flights which take an hour to get to, last ten seconds yet somehow make a serious dent in your credit card, and that's before we've bought the digital pics, the DVD, the T-shirt, and the pizza afterwards. 'I just wanted him to be cool among his friends,' winces Linda, mother of Rory, fourteen, 'and somehow the pain of the bill was dulled by the look of awe on the faces of the other kids. What will their parents top that with, I thought!'

Perhaps they'll do it with a limo. Of course, *you* know they are insufferably naff, but children never did have much taste, did they? And won't it look great when it turns up to take them all out? Beth wasn't impressed. 'My eight-year-old was invited to a private members' club in the middle of South Kensington and the mother was curiously insistent that we got there at 2.45. I thought there might be a time limit, but it turned out that there had been two classes of party invitations and there had already been a party in the morning. The second wave had to be there on time to be the welcoming party on the pavement as the limo pulled up with the more favoured friends on their way back from the morning jamboree.'

'They make more sense,' justifies a London limo company. 'If you are taking lots of kids to ice skating or bowling then one big car means you don't have to have lots of mothers delivering children.' But, it admits, people book cars in their fleet for a three-hour drive around to look at the sights (you could get halfway to Scotland in that time) and drink pop and eat in the back. You can pack in twenty-six little friends in a Hummer (four flat-screen TVs and a mirrored ceiling if the view gets boring) and it would be a snip at £685.

Wow! Any more? 'Well, we took fifteen fourteen- and fifteen-year-olds to paint balling the other day and their dad wanted the limo to stick around.' So while they splattered paint at each other the car sat there then brought them back again at a cool £1,285 for a six-hour hire. If that wasn't enough, it delivered them to a restaurant (fifteen kids remember), then presumably there were taxis home. You do the maths.

Well, at least there wouldn't have been any booze, them being under age and all. Forget it. While it's illegal for these companies to allow kids to drink while they are unaccompanied, put a parent there and a crate of alcopops and that's okay.

As boundaries have slackened so the teenage party becomes more an exercise in crowd control and the vice squad. We seem to have completely forgotten the boundaries our parents set for our parties – were we that hard done by? – and have a very tenuous hold indeed on the whole event.

'I can't believe myself,' says Sarah, whose daughter Anna is fifteen. 'I was brought up in a house where we weren't allowed to have friends around on a Sunday because it was quiet family time and here I am creeping downstairs to the sitting room at 3 a.m. when my daughter has friends over and bleating, "Soo sorry to interrupt but would you mind quietening down a teensy bit cos I'm trying to sleep."'

The sleepover party (or the no-sleepover) is one of the more irritating bloody things we have inherited from the States, along with baby showers and Mary Kate and Ashley. Didn't we used to just 'stay the night at someone's house'? So why this silly cute word? And sleep has nothing to do with it. When you finally get the horde into some sort of order, after they have trashed your sitting room watching *Legally Blonde* and getting high on Skittles and Pringles (then demanding toast) you then spend the next three hours trying to get a bit of quiet, aware that it will embarrass everyone if you lose your temper and get firm – they might dislike you, heaven forbid!

'We were woken at 2 a.m.,' remembers Ally, 'when a

girl burst into our room asking if I had any eye make-up remover!' And she probably found herself sheepishly getting some for her. Then it gets to 3 a.m. and you have a total sense of humour failure and let rip at 50 decibels, shocking the little sods into silence. As you drag yourself from your bed next morning, feeling as if you have been hit by a train, you vow that never ever again will you have anyone to stay over.

But, like childbirth, somehow you forget the pain and find yourself planning another one . . .

Even the sleepover is just about bearable if the only drink involved is Diet Coke. Alcohol is a whole new ball game. 'We were so naïve,' admits Lyn. 'When our daughter had her fifteenth birthday we said we weren't providing drink but they could bring some if they wanted to, and we imagined it would be wine and a bit of beer. Oh yeah? There was champagne, whisky, brandy, vodka. At about 1 a.m. a boy passed out and I called his mother. "Oh, he's allergic to alcohol," she told me. "If I'd known there was going to be drink I wouldn't have let him come!" At my younger daughter, Joey's, party I was wiser and frisked everyone when they arrived! I am amazed by how little other parents ask details about parties. It's either ignorance or laziness. When she was fourteen, Joey was invited to a sleepover party at a hotel in Eastbourne owned by the hostess's grandmother. Will you be there? I asked her mother. "Oh, I hadn't thought about that," she replied, and when I asked her how she was going to stop them all sleeping together, she said, "Well, you have to trust them some time." I didn't let her go.'

Ali thought her son Jake, fourteen, was at a New Year's Eve party in Brighton with the parents there until she got a call from outside a nightclub at 2 a.m. where he was throwing up his guts. Where was the host's mother? Goodness knows, but, says Ali, I had to believe her when she said she'd stay there with them. What else could I do?'

We aren't the first generation to fret about teenage parties – though I think when we were younger it was cider not Bacardi Breezers and spliffs – but where we differ from our parents is that we are so self-conscious or keen to be seen as chilled and uninterfering that we don't even bother to check what the children are going to be up to. 'I think we want to be considered cool,' says Jane, mother of Angus and Tom, sixteen and fourteen, 'which is odd when we spend so much time when they are little fretting about how safe they are. One minute we're not letting them play in the woods in case they hurt themselves or are abducted by some deranged murderer, and the next, as they become teenagers, we do the reverse and let them go out until all hours when the dangers are much more real. It's nuts!'

Ben, dad of Ed and Chloe, finds it hard. 'To maintain control is hard work. I can see why my dad insisted we were home by midnight – he wanted to go to bed. Now you have to be up till 3 a.m. when they get back and I can't be bothered. I have to admit I just close my eyes and hope to God they are being sensible.'

Mummy says I had a lovely time

And does any of this party angst get rewarded? Not likely. Have you noticed the way the thank you letter, like butter puff biscuits and Parma violets, has almost completely disappeared? While Boxing Day was once the worst day of the year as you were made to sit down and write to Aunty Mary to thank her for the Kerplunk game, you now find yourself looking back on it fondly. At least then we knew how to be grateful and now, on the rare occasions a thank you letter does arrive, it's like winning the Premium Bonds. So why aren't we making our children write them? 'Ah, no one does that any more,' says some achingly self-conscious thirteen-year-old, so you don't push the point because the last thing you want is for him to arrive at school with a pile of letters in neatly addressed envelopes and look geeky.

So, phew, at least that's it until next year. Just one thing: you have booked the venue, haven't you?

Many happy returns.

New types of party parties

Proms: that other irritating import from the US, and they don't just happen at the end of school life: there are proms at the end of the school year, the end of term, even at half-term probably. You trawl Topshop with your daughter holding up possible outfits for her sneering opinion, and she shakes her head in disbelief and continues to go through the T-shirt rail. But it doesn't just stop at the outfit. 'When your teenager gets invited to the school prom,' urges the dedicated party planning company, 'the last thing you want is for her to walk down the stairs in the expensive outfit you bought for her, looking like Magenta from the *Rocky Horror Show*!!! – Why not invite her friends around for the afternoon and have their make-up applied professionally and their hair styled – they will feel like the belle of the ball.' Well, that's something else to organise. And then there's the After Prom party. Time to hit Topshop again.

Halloween: what used to be the biggest non-event of the year now involves buying an outfit in Tesco with a range of plastic teeth and face paints that has been on display since the Easter egg range came down. Then there is the trick or treating, which anyone over the age of twenty thinks is nonsense, but we still find ourselves forking out four quid for a pumpkin and handing out Haribo to grasping little children who are clueless about what it's all about and actually think it's called 'trickle treat'.

Baby Showers: oh, come on. It's just an excuse for more presents.

Sixteenth Birthday Parties: these are on a par with the eighteenth and twenty-first in case they can't wait that long. Be careful you don't peak too early because where can you go from here?

Extreme Parties

'We once did a bar mitzvah for a hundred and twenty guests, twenty-five of whom were children. We did an upmarket music theme all in black and white. We made every table look like a grand piano. By the time we had installed the set, the forty-piece orchestra had flown in specially from Israel, the kids' table was already an afterthought and the budget – probably in excess of £100,000. Then we did a christening party for a one-year-old which was a Wild West Town complete with rodeo!'

Gary, party planner

4
School Entry: Admission Impossible

So we've got our prototype, and it's looking pretty fantastic. All that careful planning has paid off. And now it's time for the product launch. And on which lucky educators will we bestow the honour of nurturing our perfect and utterly gifted child? It's only a matter of time, surely, before they will be forming an orderly queue outside our house.

Hey, babe, wake up and smell the espresso. Getting our children into the *right* school these days is about as traumatic and complicated as swimming the Channel with your arms tied. In fact, in the face of huge demand for places and catchment area border disputes that make the Gaza Strip question look simple, there's not even any guarantee we will be able to get them into the *wrong* school.

Be under no illusion: when it comes to school entry, this is war. 'You're in it for the long haul,' says one battle-scarred veteran. There are no tactics, no dirty tricks to which we will not descend and the most alarming part of all is that casualties are usually the result of friendly fire and wholesale treachery. We think our friends are allies because they are on the same side, all united against the enemy – the massed opposition that is the admissions appeal committee. Don't you believe it.

And all this warmongering seems to bring out traits in our personalities that we never imagined were there. 'You say you won't be like that, but you are,' says another casualty. 'Something takes over. A certain madness will descend, and every principle that you have ever held dear will be abandoned.' It reveals levels of dishonesty that we won't contemplate employing anywhere else in our lives: we lie, cheat, play the wild card to get our offspring into the right seat of education, using espionage and subterfuge that would have made the KGB blush. The loss of perspective is terminal.

But can't they see how special we are?

Oh, the shamelessness of it all, because this ugly dogfight is not just to secure that last desk in the superest-dooperest school in the county so our children get the very best. It's about naked competition. It's about pimping ourselves and our families, because we're worth it (and therefore worth more than everybody else).

Naturally, whoever teaches our child will rapidly realise they're dealing with someone very special indeed. They'll never have seen such aptitude before – or such steely determination. And that's only us, the parents, we're talking about. Our main role as a parent right from the word go is as a facilitator and opportunity-provider in an ever more competitive world. We all know that if we play our cards right and choose the right pre-school, our children will be set fair for the best primary school, the finest secondary education, a first-class degree at a venerable university and a high-rolling job in the City.

But if we get it wrong . . . Well, the best our children can ever hope for is a fistful of ASBOs and a job flipping burgers while waiting for a lucky break working as a drug dealer. They will have miserable lives, and *we* will be to blame. We realize they can't all be winners. Some will lose. But it won't be ours.

So hurry up, there's no time to waste. The world is full of dangers and nasty rough people, so the sooner we can put some distance between our cosy little nuclear family and the great unwashed the better. Six-year-olds can take GCSEs now, A levels at eleven, then off to university at twelve, and then . . . Well, we'll have to think about that when the time comes, cos right now we're far too busy stimulating that beautiful little mind. Before long, our children will earn enough to look after us in our penniless dotage, once we've squandered every penny on their education.

Milestones or Millstones?

This pursuit of perfection starts early with the purchase of those educational mobiles, rattles and brightly coloured plastic structures that will dominate our home for the first few years.

It's not until we come out into baby society, like a blushing debutante at her first ball, with our brand-new change bag and pristine car seat, that we really become aware that we have been slow out of the stalls. We may have suspected, of course, because those blasted baby books had planted the seed of self-doubt, but now we know for sure. Because there are lots of people out there to tell us how they are already around the first bend.

'I went to an NCT member's house for a coffee morning,' remembers Rachel, 'and, taped all over the house, were these handwritten cards – door, chair, window. Our babies were four months old. But I was so freaked out, I went home and did the same myself. When my husband got back from work, he laughed himself silly.'

The pressure's on, isn't it? Despite our better judgement and despite all the things we may have said while we were pregnant, we find ourselves comparing our baby with every other baby we see. And suddenly, things like being able to roll over or playing with toes become pivotal to our very existence. And when it comes to walking and talking! Show me a baby that can walk at ten months at toddler group and I'll show you a dozen women who go home and spend the rest of the day urging their bendy-legged bundle to stand up and go it alone, without recourse to furniture. By the time they go to school, most children are walking and talking – aren't they? – so what's with the panic? Why do we lose our perspective? When did the developmental milestones become millstones?

Implicit in the achievements of other babies is some sort of reproach to your ability as a parent. What? You mean you haven't been stimulating your baby with vivid mono-chrome mobiles? You haven't been playing classical music to increase his IQ? You haven't been chugging fish oil capsules to enhance your breast milk? Of course, that

'I know, darling, it is tricky, but you do need
a second language for St Margaret's'

explains why he's a week behind the charts in being able to sit up. What have you been doing with your time for goodness sake? Wasting it away on cuddles and 'This little piggy'? Didn't you know a baby's brain doubles in size in the first year? Well, you might as well forget Oxbridge, then, because it's probably already too late.

'I thought Debbie was my best mate,' says Sam, 'and then we had children. Her daughter was always way ahead of my son and I'd be eaten up with jealousy and practise propping him up with cushions to make it look like he could sit up. Then, ha! He said "Mama" before she did. Eat my dust, sucker!'

Forget, for a moment, the fact that Einstein was a late developer; we must leave no stone unturned in our quest to enhance baby's mind at this crucial time. Fortunately, there are plenty of products to feed into our paranoia. And all created by experts. Now we can plonk our baby in front of the telly with a clear conscience, with DVDs like *Baby Einstein*, *Baby Genius*, *Baby Shakespeare*, *Baby Van Gogh*. They're never too young to learn. And we're never too old to be taken in by a new marketing ploy!

Nursery Crimes

Always assuming that we haven't been bludgeoned into submission by Steve Biddulph's propaganda, and are actually contemplating sending our child to nursery, we now have to choose the right place.

'I looked for a nursery when I went back to work,' explains Debbie, 'for my two-year-old and found what I thought was a really lovely place. Homely, welcoming, good Ofsted report, all that sort of thing. And then another mum said, "What second language do they teach?" And I couldn't believe she was serious. The child could barely speak English!'

Just like in Lake Woebegone, every child must now be above average. So instead of being allowed to play and actually have some fun, they are assessed for pencil grip, knowing their colours, ability to sit nicely at circle time – and so much more. It's like a production line, isn't it? Well, we'd better get used to it, because that's what education has become, with our child as guinea pig, being tested, assessed and judged from now on.

'I wanted my daughter to get into a very popular private school and the competition was fierce,' says Melanie. 'So I had to send her, at the ripe old age of three and a quarter, to be assessed there, and all I was thinking was, How can I get the highest mark out of her? We were not allowed in to witness the test, but obviously they're not doing algebra, so how are they judging these little toddlers?' You wouldn't credit it – one nervous child, when asked what blue and yellow makes, blurted, 'Blellow!'

Melanie continues: 'We tried not to worry our daughter, but the night before she had a huge tanty about what she was going to wear. So I put her in the car seat and drove her round for a couple of hours, just so she would go to sleep. I felt I couldn't leave it to chance because this is how the rest of her life, her future, is basically decided.'

The teachers are in the perfect position to witness the

lunacy of potential parents from close quarters. One teacher at a minor prep school remembers showing a father around. 'He was very insistent that his son should be fast-tracked. He kept stressing how bright he was and, basically, trying to get me to agree that we would move him through the school at an accelerated pace. I asked a bit more, and eventually it came down to when he might want to start in the school. That was when he told me his son was only six months old!'

This is just the start of a long campaign to get it right, but everybody else we know is at it too. Previously amicable dinner parties suddenly become a minefield of taboo subjects. You find yourself keeping your cards close to your chest. Or, worse, intentionally feeding false information to the enemy – I mean the other guests. Don't let on that little Flossie's Japanese tuition has paid off handsomely – the head was soooo impressed at interview – or that you've just exchanged contracts on a house three inches inside the catchment for Sunnydale Junior. Everything on a need-to-know basis only.

Primary school

Back in the good old days, before league tables, our main concern about primary school would probably have been how convenient it was to get to. But now there are some schools that are so desirable, some parents will stop at nothing to try to get their precious darlings in. It's like everyone in the neighbourhood trying to squeeze into the same hypertrendy restaurant on a Saturday night. But if we go somewhere else, are we really going to end up getting a bad meal?

'When my son was eight months old,' says Amelia, mother to Harry and foetus Piers, 'we thought we'd be efficient and sign him up for a school around the corner – a very exclusive school. And they virtually laughed in our faces and said we were far too late, and the waiting list was already closed. And they suggested – quite straight-faced – that what some parents do is to get pregnant, register the unborn baby, and then our son could come in as a sibling.'

So just how low would we now sink to get our child into the primary school of our choice? According to the BBC almost a third of head teachers in the highest-ranking state primary schools have been offered bribes or threatened by parents desperate for a place for their child. Of course, we could always move house – if we can afford to. The effect of a good school on house prices within the catchment area is staggering. It is featured prominently on house sale details even outside London. Sod the ensuite, what makes a res des these days is how close it is to the school gates. Trouble is, the catchment area keeps getting smaller and smaller – down to less than half a mile in some places *as the crow flies* – as all the local properties are snapped up by hopeful parents.

'My children went to a nursery based at the local state primary school,' says John, a desperate parent. 'The problem was that the nursery had twice as many places as the reception class, so basically half the children at the nursery wouldn't get a place. We used to scour the streets for removal vans, wondering if someone was going to move in with twins, closer to the school than we were, and rob my kids of their place in the school. It was a traumatic two years. The children are supposed to be enjoying playing with sand and splashing around with water while all the parents going home are weeping because their children aren't going to get into this school.'

The alternative is basically to lie about where we live. And plenty of people try it, giving a false address, or renting a tiny flat next to the school while keeping a nice big house elsewhere. Schools and education authorities are on to them, though, running checks through the electoral register.

'Two children had to leave the school because their parents had given a false address,' says Gerard, father of two. 'It was awful. The parents were called in and confronted with the evidence. They just disappeared. No one saw them again. Maybe they were sent to the salt mines. But nobody cared because it meant that two more places were available.'

A head teacher of a very popular state school says, 'All the effort these parents go to! If they sent their children to schools that still have places, and used even a fraction of the energy and determination they show trying to get into a school that's full, they could support the head and teachers, and the school would improve. Of course it would.'

Pray or pay?

But if we're not in the catchment area, and we're not ready to hand out bribes or invent a bogus address just yet, what's left? There are two strategic options. We either sell everything we own and go private, or we get religion, and fast. But not just a little religion, as Lucy saw at first hand.

'Just going to church at Christmas and Easter isn't good enough any more and wearing a little cross round your neck won't convince anyone. So my sister did the full going to Sunday school, going to church, being terribly helpful with the flower-arranging and all that kind of thing. She roped us all in, the entire family running stalls at the church fête to get the child into school. And it worked.'

And if you are a bogus born-again, be sure your sin will find thee out. In one popular Catholic school, baptismal certificates had to be called in to check that children had in fact been baptised before they had applied to the school. Several places became available after that. Rumbled!

So if we can't square a sudden conversion with our conscience, and no other school will do or have you, all that's left is to pay and just tough it out. And once we leave the state system, it can be hard to get back in until senior school entry comes along.

'I've had to do the lottery, stay up late doing Internet poker games, go to car boot sales and become familiar with eBay,' says a poor private parent. 'We live from term to term, not really knowing if they'll be able to go back. I do realise that this is true madness. But there doesn't seem to be an alternative round here.'

And this is all before the poor little thing has even turned five. 'There's the moment when we get our child into the nursery school or primary school of our choice,' says John. 'There's a sort of brief moment of elation – five minutes, tops – followed by a growing anxiety as the years rush past and we start to worry more and more about the next big hurdle: getting into secondary school.'

This is when we need to radio in for back-up.

Coaching for the slowcoach

At one time, having extra tutoring was regarded as a shameful secret – a bit like having webbed feet. But now at least one in four families in the UK gets coaching for their children in something or another. To pile on the pressure, there are always stories in the newspapers about freaky six-year-olds passing their GCSEs. There are even crammers that specialise in this kind of mental torture. And although we can see it's weird and wrong, a part of us has the uncomfortable feeling that maybe we should be doing the same for our child. Anything if it will help secure a place at the right school.

And as our kids get older, the pressure builds up these days. While selective state schools continue to exist, the iniquity of coaching for secondary school entry will continue and parents feel under huge pressure to coach because everybody else does. Some fee-paying primary schools seem to function as eleven-plus factories for grammar schools, charging a fortune to shove children through the entrance exams just to save the parents the money they would have spent on school fees for the senior years. Hmm – makes you think. Because state primary schools don't have the time to cram their pupils in this way, private tutors can clean up. One tutor notes, 'Generally a child needs at least two years' preparation for the exam. At £10 per hour, twice a week, that can cost over £2,000. But it's a lot less than paying for private school.'

Some parents will consider going even further with this madness. One father advertised recently on the Internet offering to pay for a copy of the entrance paper his daughter was due to take. The school found out and were not at all impressed. But what's the point? Many teachers are of the opinion that coaching distorts the whole system.

'If a child can't pass the exam without a lot of help, then they would be better suited to an education elsewhere. It wouldn't be fair on them to put them in an environment where they're struggling to keep up with their peers,' says one head teacher.

But parents are unrepentant. 'It's all a game, isn't it? But it's not a game – it's the World Cup!' says Darren shamelessly.

'Secondary school, we'll do anything basically. We'll do anything, whatever it takes,' Trevor says. 'It's not a level playing field any more. All these schools have got their good points and bad points. I'll do anything to get them in. It's a very, very, very good school. Too good for our kids to go to actually but I don't care, I'll do anything.'

Gerard knew that an early start was essential.

Bribery and extortion

It's not just the heads who are worth corrupting, of course. Bribery can work with children too and, when the stakes are so high, a decent bribe for passing the entrance exam is well worth offering. Trouble is there are no rules for where to pitch it.

'When I found out my son had passed his eleven-plus, I got him a great big ice cream. Then we met a girl who'd been promised that she could have her belly button pierced if she passed, and another kid who was bought a pony!' Jacqui laughs.

Schools are very well aware of the panic we succumb to. And if we hedge our bets and apply to private schools as well as state, there's a price to pay.

'For each private school we apply to, there's a fee to take the entrance exam and a non-returnable deposit. And we have to hand this over, of course, before we hear which state school our child has been accepted into,' laments Justine. 'It cost me hundreds, literally hundreds of pounds, just to keep our options open.'

There's a strange sort of tension that arises between state and private parents and those who go the grammar school route. There are undercurrents that can test the most established friendships. Our choice of school says so much about our worldview and it polarises people in the last couple of years at primary school. Suddenly you find yourself cosying up with the parents of kids who are applying to the same schools as you are – because someone you once liked has taken the traitor route and gone private. Adversity makes strange bedfellows.

Unappealing Parents

Despite government claims about now giving parents more choice, tens of thousands of children do not get places at the school their parents want for them. So what happens next? Don't take it lying down, brave warrior.

Some parents are paying hundreds of pounds to consultants because they are desperate to win their school appeals. Rather than taking no for an answer, and accepting that the school is full, they will challenge the decision and try to force their way in. Consultants offer their services, at a price, and claim they can increase the success rate of appeals from about 15 per cent unassisted to as much as 70 per cent. For an extra consideration, they will even appear at the appeals alongside the parents.

But would you want to be the parent who pushes the class size over the critical number? The crazy part is in state primary schools in particular, where class numbers for the early years are dictated by the government, just having one extra child can force the school to split the class and employ another teacher.

Susie remembers feeling resentful. 'We had these parents who pushed and pushed, and their appeals were granted. The class size was just too big. It meant the classroom was overcrowded and all our kids, who'd been there since the start, got less attention. It just seemed really selfish. We all used to glare at the parents in the playground. I don't think they noticed. They were so chuffed to have beaten the system.'

Best days of our life?

After living and breathing school entry for what feels like years and years, we finally get our child in somewhere or other. And if we end up just accepting the place we're allocated, it might turn out to be better than we feared.

'We gave up eventually and I remember thinking, Oh, well, I think this school will suit them perfectly after all, and everyone can relax and feel a bit happier,' says a resigned mother. 'We stopped hating our child, finally, after this long campaign, our child who was never good enough for a scholarship somewhere or a special place somewhere else. And then it begins again for another set of parents; the following year we're at the school gates with our younger kids and we hear them talking, and we know the hell they're going through. They're going to suffer exactly the same way that we did. They look for advice – we're reluctant to give it. Even after we got that place we don't want to share our information.'

The gamesmanship doesn't let up as the years go by. Another wave of lunacy takes over between GCSEs and A levels, when those of us who've slogged to get our children into lovely, privileged private schools suddenly get a wake-up call. Because of recent positive discrimination for the scallys from state schools, our cossetted darlings may not be able to swan into the uni of their choice. The solution? We hoick our kids out of private school at sixteen, then send them to state school to sit A levels. The children will already have benefitted from an elite education for most of their schooldays, and can probably withstand having to study with the common people for a couple of years. The university admissions officers, however, will assume they have spent all their academic life in a 'bog-standard comp' and will allocate their places accordingly. We just have to hope their cut-glass accents won't give the game away at interview. Estuary elocution lessons, anyone? The rine in Spine . . .

University challenged

So we've barged our kids through the education system as fast as we can. University awaits our under-aged boff and, with it, the reflected glory that the parents of a freakishly brilliant child can bask in. All those sacrifices we've had to make for our moment in the sun. But brace yourself: Oxford is considering a minimum age limit of seventeen as a response to child protection laws. So while we're waiting, our tiny genius will have to cool their heels and take another batch of A levels while learning to play the cor anglais, just to while away the years.

All that effort for nothing. And was it worth it? Will they thank us in the end? Alex doesn't think so. 'Sometimes, in a rare moment of sanity, I compare Jack's life to mine when I was a child. I wouldn't like to have his life. I'm always on his case about working harder. But I'm like that because everyone else is too. It's no wonder that children love books with heroes like Pippi Longstocking,

Harry Potter and Alex Rider. They're all orphans who can do what they like without parents bossing them around.'

A Dozen Daft Names

The following have appeared at least once among the 600,000 births registered in Britain over the past twelve months.

For her . . .
Ikea
Paprica
Caramel
Bambi
Fire-Lily
Skylark

For him . . .
Moet
Finchley
Ely
Rocky
Rivers
Red

5
School Life: Forgery and Fraud

Of course getting our children into the chosen school is just the start of fourteen years of obsession. And obsession it is. School talk dominates dinner parties, benches at the park, chats over a latte in Starbucks. There are forums on the Internet about it. It makes you wonder what we all talked about before. Babies probably.

Having children in school is a funny old feeling, isn't it? You probably haven't been near a school gate for fifteen years or so and suddenly, instead of being there as a pupil, you are delivering your offspring. The odd part is you have a mixture of emotions: the teachers still manage to make you feel as though, if you misbehave, you will be sent to see the head. The smell of a pencil case, the beautifully written labels next to the pegs, the cabbagey waft of school dinners. It all takes you back to those days of short trousers or long white socks, and you feel cowed and small again.

Then you remind yourself that the teachers are probably younger than you are.

Sending our children off to school brings out a whole new side to our personalities, and we become people we don't recognise. Granted we have moved house, lied, scraped or re-mortgaged even to get him into the place

anyway and we are, after all, handing over our pride and joy to someone else for about thirty-nine weeks of the year, so a little concern and involvement is natural. But instead of giving up our children to education on trust, it is here that modern parenting shows new heights of insanity.

'Teaching is the only profession where other people think they know best,' sighs Margaret, a pre-prep head with years of teaching experience at a private school. 'I mean, you don't appoint an accountant and then tell him how to do his job, or tell the dentist how to do an extraction. Parents these days are not in the real world. In the last ten years there's been a sea change in the way parents behave and it's warping the children's minds.'

'Government Guff', as she calls it, is partly to blame, and who can resist being alarmed by a feature on low-performing schools and the threat that your child is being sold short? There's a bit of jealousy there too: galling, isn't it, that your son's teacher might just know a side of him you don't? Suddenly he's learning things not from us but from someone else. But the real problem is that schools have become a service industry and we treat them like car dealerships.

State versus private

Which ones of us are the worst then? Those of us who pay or those of us who move heaven and earth to be in the right catchment area for St Top-of-the-League-Tables? Private school parents, in response to the pain that results from paying through the nose, very definitely expect a return for their investment these days. And why shouldn't we? At the current rate – not allowing for inflation – we're forking out enough during their school careers to buy a small three-bedroom house. You can double that and a bit more if you take the boarding school route. Not surprising then that you want to make darned sure Jimmy is going to 'realise his potential'. And, while you're at it, the certainty of a lucrative job in the City or a partnership in the top law firm would be very nice too. So, just to make quite sure that's the way things are heading, we behave as if our children were comestibles.

'I was taking register one morning,' continues Margaret, 'and the door was thrown open by a mother, her face purple with anger. "Are you teaching my child nothing?" she shrieked. "Am I wasting my money here!"' It transpired it was all about a piece of extra homework she had demanded her child be given, which he had then refused to do. 'It's all about value for money.'

'One mother,' relates another long-experienced teacher, 'asked if she could have a video camera in the classroom so she could watch her child in school. Strangely enough we said no!'

But unlike a BMW, whereby the more you spend the higher the spec, it doesn't quite work that way with children. A few grand and your daughter's exceptional ability at drawing may not be enough to ensure she turns out a genius.

Margaret sees this pattern of expectation all the time: 'I had to tell one father that his son was not doing very well. "I'm amazed you are telling me the truth," he said. "I thought if I was paying for his schooling you would put a gloss on it"!'

What we don't seem to want to accept is that we can throw all the money we like at school and education, but it won't make our children any more intelligent.

In state schools, we are just as pushy but in a subtly different way. It's the 'it's my right' mentality. We know that Barny might just develop later and we should leave him to find his way, but we can't resist, can we? We have to know where he is *now* in relation to other children. 'He's doing okay,' simply isn't a good enough answer, is it? We need to know success is happening already.

But what both payers and non-payers have in common is this growing 'parents versus the school' attitude. 'Letters from solicitors,' groans the head of the comprehensive in the north-east. 'I never used to get them before. Now I receive about two a week.'

They are usually growling threats of litigation, another influence from America no doubt, but the demands we place on schools seem to have got more absurd by the minute. At the lowest level we want them to potty-train our children and teach them how to hold a knife and fork. 'They've been so coached to perform at home before they start nursery that some can write their own names when they come in,' says one teacher, 'but they can't eat lunch. What on earth are the parents doing?'

At best we want results; at worst we want teachers to do our job for us. But it all gets a bit more sinister when it comes to playtime.

Where there's blame, there's a claim

Blame it on the Yanks, but we seem to have become obsessed with wrapping our children in cotton wool to the point that has made litigants of us all. Nothing new here of course – we've been an increasingly blame and compensation culture for a while now. Trip over a paving stone in the street and you can be sure your case will be taken on by a firm of lawyers advertising on daytime TV, who'll take the local council to the cleaners.

Trouble is the councils and, ergo, schools are now so terrified of legal action from us parents that they are banning anything that could be faintly contentious. Take playground games. There we are on one hand saying, 'Oh, it isn't like the old days, is it, when we used to string rubber bands together and play skipping games, or British Bulldog – remember that? Kids these days – no idea how to entertain themselves and have fun.' And then what do we do? Issue proceedings against the school because Annabel slipped and grazed her knee.

Unfortunately we can't go blaming other parents here. A Mori poll suggests that if their child suffered personal injury at school that they felt to be the fault of the school or school staff, then the majority of parents would seek compensation from the school. In fact only 15 per cent said they would never consider doing this.

Dr Sarah Thomson from the Education Department of Keele University published a report recently after studying three primary schools across three counties. She found that British Bulldog was banned in all schools; and conkers were viewed as offensive weapons. 'I even heard one member of staff talk about banning conkers because she linked conkers with nuts, which might expose children to nut allergies.'

Instead of sticking on a plaster, teachers now have to tell a child to dab a cut with a wet paper towel; well, imagine the consequences if the child proved to be allergic to Elastoplast. (Wouldn't you let the school know if your child was?) One school in Thomson's study had even banned skipping after some girls had tied their legs together with ropes for a three-legged race, and subsequently fallen over.

Suddenly, says Thomson, 'the children's choice of pastime and amusement must be regulated for both the teachers' and the children's protection.'

'We could not do otherwise,' says one head, 'or you are leaving yourself open. You say you are *in loco parentis* but really you are not. You have to ask permission to do anything, everything.'

Another head teacher admitted that he would like to 'ban all playtimes, as they are a nightmare'.

Is there something wrong with children these days? Do they have thinner skin or brittler bones? The crazy part is that Thomson observed 'many of the children's attempts to play were extinguished by the same supervising adults who complained that children "did not play".'

'We played British Bulldogs and we nearly killed each other,' one says, 'but that was the object! Children get hurt. We used to get hurt when we were playing it. People used not to bother in those days. I think we are much more safety-conscious; we can't let children just play anything nowadays.'

How many children do you know who have suffered dreadful injuries from conker fights or ingesting Top Trump cards? Our concern with safety has reached frankly barking proportions. Sure, there is the theoretical possibility that little Jimmy might just get a bit of conker in his eye/fall over and break his ankle/get a runny nose from the cold and, for some reason, that seems to be sufficient risk to justify the call for a ban. Our demands for bans (or at least the school's decision to ban it in case of our response to accidents) are triggered by the *potential* risk that something might happen, and not by specific evidence that it has. Frankly there is more danger in driving them to school in your car (instead of letting them walk – but that's another story).

This 'us versus the school' attitude is even more divisive than nasty letters from Sue Them & Win. 'The whole mood has changed,' says one head. 'If something happens in class and I have to tell a child off – sometimes for something quite serious – I get the parents on my back the next morning. What happened to children's accountability? There is always an excuse. Their little darling can't possibly have done something wrong and how dare we tell him or her off? Parents seem to build a defence mechanism around their children and we are always on the back foot. They never seem to be able to say sorry, either, when they have clearly got something wrong.'

Will you join the committee?

You might be the sort of person who would rather have their skull drilled than join a committee of any kind, but it all changes, doesn't it, when there's a chance of getting a closer look at school life and a peek at what other kids are up to. There only has to be a whiff of involvement – make-up for the school play, reading help in class, baking cakes for the fête – and we can get that foot in the door and closer to the coalface.

Until that moment the only insight we had was the school bag of a child who came back with yours for tea. There it is by the front door, crying out for you to have a peek and, unable to resist and while their backs are turned as they watch *CBeebies*, you open it up. If you are lucky you can sit back on your heels in smug satisfaction as you see they have read far fewer books than your child. There are his mother's excuses: 'Dan was tired tonight.' Dan may be seven but, you hope, that one night's missed reading might be the difference between an A and a B at GCSE. The pleasure.

But there's always the risk of the terror. The Superstar stamp from the teacher to congratulate Dan on finishing *War and Peace*. And, worse still, there's the News Book, that most insidious of tomes that reveals all about someone else's family life you never see. Trips to National Trust properties and art galleries. Culture made fun.

Ilana couldn't resist a nose when a friend came over: 'I had a little sneaky peek inside the book bag and sure enough there were the most amazing Miró illustrations of what they'd done at the weekend. My kid does things like go to a car wash and Asda shopping, so there was quite a discrepancy and also in the quality of the work. With my kid each letter was apart and this child was already doing joined-up writing aged four. It wasn't a very happy experience, I must admit, but the problem was I forgot to actually put the book back in the book folder and in fact the mother had to phone me about three nights later and say, "Have you got Xander's exercise book?"'

Get through the classroom door, though, and you can really make comparisons. 'I definitely went in to help with reading so I could see how Katie was doing compared to the class,' admits Hannah. 'You can only find out so much from the book bag, but being in class was brilliant!'

John has a theory about this: 'They're not listening to the child read – they've got the other ear firmly cocked in the direction of the class round the corner, seeing what is being taught; whether their child was left unattended for a microsecond and, you know, all that intelligence is gathered and taken back home and collated, and probably they're gonna be a governor of the school as well so that will be brought up at the governors' meetings. And sometimes there are so many parents going in to volunteer to read in some of these classrooms that there's no chance of any children being left in the actual classroom to be taught by the teacher, because the parents are too busy spying on them!'

Why can't we resist the snooping? Ilana is honest: 'I couldn't accept that another child was so much better than my child,' she admits. Jane, however, justifies her

'*Don't* get little Henry started on the causes
of the First World War . . .'

involvement. 'Of course you want to get in there. My daughter is in a school in Islington where the teacher can't even spell! I know that if I can get myself in the classroom I can have some sort of understanding of what's going on.'

Day Tripping

It doesn't even have to be the PTA committee or the reading help; it could just be the school outing, that wonderful opportunity to see your child in relation to others and you've got the whole day to do it. It's always the same mothers and fathers who go, though, isn't it? The type who like to be right up there on the good egg ratings, turning up in anorak, sensible shoes, with a few treats in their backpack for the children in their group (that'll make them popular with their children's friends). It all looks suspiciously like information-gathering tactics hidden beneath a helpful and altruistic veneer.

So we are nosey and we are controlling. We are also paranoid and, when our children are taken out of school, that safety obsession becomes pure madness. In fact in one Midlands primary school a trip to a science museum had to be cancelled when there were too many parents volunteering to go and not enough space on the bus, but none would yield and back down.

One teacher recently gave up the profession, so exhausted was he by paranoid parenting. He wearily recalls how another school trip to the seaside, planned for a class of five-year-olds, was cancelled because two parents were concerned that the trip would involve their children in a forty-minute journey in a private car. Would the cars be fully MOT-ed? Were they good enough drivers? Who would ensure correct-fitting seat belts? Were these normally non-smoking cars, or would the children be made victims of passive smoking?

One child's parents even booked a holiday cottage down the road from a school trip destination so they could keep a beady eye and another's mother insisted on driving behind her son's coach on a trip to France to ensure that he arrived safely.

'Can you promise,' insisted one mother at a pre-ski trip meeting at school, 'that someone will come down the piste with Olivia each time to check she is okay?'

Prep and homework

If you can't make your way in through the school trip or PTA routes, the most useful clue to what's going on in school is homework. It's also the most stressful.

Children seem to come home with prep – even if it's in the form of a repetitive and tedious reading book – from the moment they start nursery. Then the amount cranks up as expected, but in the primary years it all seems a little *de trop*. Why do schools feel the children need this much?

The truth is they don't. It's parents who demand it and extra work to boot. 'Even when the child is as young as three, parents want to know where the reading book is,' says Margaret, but it's essential. It's vital. Imagine the ignominy if your child is a level behind the rest of his peers on the Magic Key series! Career disaster; and extra work is even more essential when you take him out of school for a week to make the most of the cheap flights to Geneva for skiing before half-term.

Then there's the Project. Don't the very words fill you with horror? At least there's the Internet so you don't have to schlep down to the library to find that someone else from school has already taken out the only book on Victorian childhood.

'I really really try not to help her,' says Jane, pained, 'but, God, I have so much to say.' And it's irresistible sometimes. Your son is flailing about for information on the economy in Spain, switching back to Runescape on the Internet when you leave the room, until you realise the night before the project is due in he's managed bullfighting and sherry, so in you wade, sleeves rolled up and best research and analysis head on.

Darren takes up the story: 'You want your child to do well at school and it's very difficult because you also want them to learn for themselves and it's so hard; it's so difficult because you're sitting there watching them make mistakes. I've spent nights sort of rubbing out her times table and rewriting them and trying to recreate her handwriting, and getting the five round the wrong way and stuff. And you think: What am I doing, what am I doing?'

Teachers aren't stupid. That's why they write WDM very small at the bottom of the page of homework – Well Done Mum. They make their way determinedly across the playground at 3.30 and pin you with a beady eye: well, did you help with the homework, only it seemed a little better than Samantha's usual standard? And, like a shoplifter faced with the store detective, you hold their eye as steady as you can and swear blind it was all her own work.

But isn't it worth it when the merit badges are handed out, though of course it's you who takes the plaudits. After all, you did most of the work. And sometimes it's not about the children at all – it's between the parents. Two fathers were locked in mortal combat over who had done the best seaside project, both producing something resembling a geologist's scale model made from papier-mâché and sand glued to dunes made painstakingly from wire and plaster, both trying to outdo each other on the exoticness of the shells glued to the shoreline, brought back, one can only assume, from competing holidays in the Caribbean.

In some sort of misguided belief that extra work, better projects, or involvement will speed them along the road to success, we persist. This must explain why we feel this urge to interfere with their education. Unless, of course, it is a desire to bask in reflected glory. If they are doing well, then aren't we the clever ones? After all, it must be genetic.

But that's if you find out a project has to be done at all. 'I don't normally get involved in their homework,' says Emma, 'but I remember coming in to collect my daughter from school on the first day back after the Easter holidays. One of the other mothers sidled up to me. "So what did you think of the holiday science project?" she asked. I could feel the cold sweat. Clemmy hadn't mentioned a science project but I couldn't admit I didn't know. I still found myself saying, "Oh that!" and thinking, *What*?'

Could do better

So how did you do? Enter the parents' evening, the most intense five – or if you are lucky ten – minutes of the year during which you have to glean everything you can about how your pride and joy is doing. You have just 600 seconds to find out everything about Hattie or Charlie's progress, and future career prospects.

'I'm like an athlete out of the blocks,' says Fiona. 'If the parents who are in with the teacher before me overstay by even a minute after the bell I start to cough and make myself obvious. They are stealing my time! Then I try to read the grades in the teacher's mark book upside down to see how Josh has done compared to the rest of the class – while the teacher tries to put their hand over the figures. If you are quick and make a mental note of the surname of the brightest boy in the class you can spot his marks pretty quickly on the list. It helps if it begins with an A.'

Simon uses management tactics. 'I try to read the teacher's face, and see what she is really trying to say. Then afterwards I forget anything good and just focus on the bad.'

It's not always obvious what the performance grading system is anyway. You can't get teachers in state schools to tell you how well your kid is doing relative to the rest of the class so you have to deduce. What's all this with the special name code? There you are being told that the children are squares, diamonds, triangles or circles, and when you are told your child is a diamond you think that sounds great – they must be the best! – until someone tells you it's in fact the bottom percentage of the class. And just when you think you've got a handle on the system, the school changes it. Next year they are jungle animals. Panthers sounds good. Don't you believe it.

But relatively speaking it's all pretty upbeat. No more 'This child is the scourge of my class. He will go nowhere in life.' In this modern climate of win, win, win, we now get fed vapid spin. Reports are the same. You can forget: 'Has no interest, makes no effort' (Mr Wolfson, physics teacher, circa 1977). Like a management appraisal, children are now graded for effort and attainment with an S for satisfactory, 2 for middle third of the class. Like GCSEs it's impossible to make comparisons if everyone's a winner. No wonder we find ourselves interrogating the teacher like the Stasi across the desk on parents' evening.

'You have to be so careful about being negative,' says Gail, a form teacher and an old hand at this parental bunfight. 'Even the worst news has to be couched in positive statements. But I don't really know why we aren't honest. It would make no difference. Parents these days have a complete inability to see anything wrong with their children. Even quite serious defects they just won't acknowledge. Staff are on the back foot all the time.'

'It all comes down to trust,' says Keith. 'There isn't as much trust between parents and teachers any more. They don't let us get on with the job. Parents used to be nervous on parents' evening but not any more. It's all guns blazing. We have a system where parents talk in the classroom one to one with the form teacher. Now I have to sit in with some of the younger teachers when certain parents come in because they don't want to be on their own with aggressive parents.'

Fair enough to be angry if we're talking about an under-performing school with unsatisfactory teaching. But Keith heads up the lower school of a £9,000 a year prep school.

Tell us there is something wrong with the child though and we will obsess. It can't be genetic – that doesn't look good on us – so if it can't actually be blamed on the school it must be an 'ic'. The hot favourite is dyslexic, then there's dyspraxic. Yes, that'll be it. Charlie isn't doing so well at maths because he has a difficulty with number blindness, and off we go to throw the best part of two and a half grand having him 'assessed'. It's that car analogy again. If there is something wrong with the product, send it to the garage to have it put right.

It's become a modern disease to find a condition, and diagnosis of an 'ic' is very reassuring. Then at dinner parties we can say, when asked how he's doing at school/rugby/further nuclear physics, 'Well, of course he's mildly (only mildly, mind) ADHD' (an honorary 'ic'). What we suspect in our heart of hearts is that he's just hard going.

'What my wife and I couldn't bear to admit,' says a substantially poorer Larry, 'is that Harry, our son, was simply *not good enough*. In fact it pains me to say it now. He struggled with maths so we took him to a trendy clinic that had been featured on TV and, after hours of tests, which involved him trying to keep his balance on a wobbly platform, they said his cerebellum was under-developed but they could fix it. It was such a relief and we drove home with a great big weight off our shoulders. But

I think both of us knew the level of the problem was negligible and in fact he was just a bit thick at maths!'

But isn't it wonderful to know their strengths and weaknesses? Doesn't it help when it comes to choosing their exam options? If you thought the child and the school do that, you are wrong. More and more of us seem to push the decision so keen are we to 'get it right'. If we could we'd even sit the blasted exams for them.

Fear not. We can. Send them in with a mobile phone and we can be right there with them, answers ready to text when they need them. Much less obvious (and significantly less dangerous) is 'helping' them with their coursework. In fact we can virtually pass the exams for them now that the potential for plagiarism in qualifications from GCSE to university degrees is now unlimited. According to a 2006 report by the Qualifications and Curriculum Authority, there are at least ten websites offering rip-off answers to coursework in every subject from GCSE to degree level.

'Coursework assignments are available on the Internet at any level and in any subject,' the report adds. 'With so much work being completed outside school, the use of such sites cannot be controlled.' A survey revealed that 93 per cent of pupils had access to the Internet at home, and therefore could link to the websites. In addition, the report says, many parents are unaware of the limits to the amount of help they can give their children with coursework, and in some cases are supplying the answers to questions. One in twenty actually drafted their children's GCSE essays.

(We're not going to reveal the websites to you of course in case your child does better than ours . . .)

PPs: Pushy parents

These are the people we love to hear about. You know the ones – the parents who go to ridiculous lengths to ensure their child achieves/gets the best/does their best. It's all the more satisfying because the things they do are perfectly barking. It couldn't be *us*. We *wouldn't* . . .

No one ever really confesses to being a pushy parent. We find ourselves couching any suggestion of over-zealousness in terms like 'helping him to achieve his potential' or 'making sure he gets the best'. Who's actually going to stand up and say, 'My son is damned well going to lick the lot of you at backstroke and we've been up at 6 a.m. pounding the pool every morning for months'? Well, no one is actually going to say it, but it's a rare one who doesn't do a little gentle directional encouragement no matter how low-key.

Overt PPs are irresistible really and you loathe them, until you find yourself signing your child up for extra violin. But you too read the article that said research shows the offspring of pushy parents are much more likely to succeed in life than those with hands-off ones. After that nugget, how can you *not* steer your progeny with a gentle but firm hand?

So you too are sucked into the PP-dom. You might be the private type, the grade one PP who tries to make sure your darling wins (sorry, fulfils his potential) with a little extra tennis coaching or the odd 'How do you spell "indiscreet"?' The grade two and three PP does the pushing in private, hoping that their efforts will pay off when the activity is done in public: the practising for the egg and spoon race on the lawn which will give them the edge on sports day, or a little extra help from a tutor to back up what they are already learning.

Every little helps

Tutoring used to be for toffs who were educated at home, away from the great unwashed. It was also for those of us who ploughed our A levels and hadn't a chance of a university place unless we miraculously converted a D in French to at least a B in re-sits. Now private tutors are everywhere and even Tony Blair is alleged to have hired one for his children. Right from Key Stage 1, we can secure them for reading, English and maths. 'Give your children an extra chance to shine,' coos one private tutor's ad.

'It's essential,' screech both Beth and Jane, north London mothers with children about to move from infants to juniors. 'It's not about outdoing everyone else in their class now. We do it because the education system has let us down. If they didn't have extra help there is no way they would be good enough to get into the best schools. What else are we supposed to do?'

That's fair enough. With teacher to pupil ratios in Britain the lowest in Europe then you need all the advantages you can get. No, we're talking people who engage tutors above and beyond the call of what could reasonably be called sane. 'We had a call recently from a mother who wanted her child to have hours of Italian classes,' recalls one firm of tutors. 'She had heard that if a child is exposed to a language early, it is easier for them to become fluent. The child turned out to be one and a half.'

On the other hand, there's always the grade four and upwards PPs who can't resist the urge to display their conscientious parenting for all to witness and it's never more overt than in the sporting arena. There they are – the mothers with their mobile phone on stopwatch checking Rebecca's time at one length front crawl. They sit in a gaggle and compare notes, explaining away poor performance with excuses about 'being tired after playing hockey for the A team yesterday'. The more single-minded pace up and down the edge of the pool screeching stirring words to the child, who can't hear them anyway over the noise of water inside their swimming cap.

'I see some odd behaviour at the swimming club,' says Ally, 'where one or two parents think their children might be good enough for national or even international level. One poor girl (who actually isn't all that good) is taken to every session: that's every evening and two 6 a.m. swims a week as well – probably ten hours a week easy. Recently she broke her arm but, amazingly, she turned up at training, holding her plastered arm out of the water as she swam!'

Tennis club reveals a rich seam of PPs too. 'We had one girl who played pretty well until she suddenly stopped coming,' says Paul, a tennis coach. 'I saw her a few weeks later and asked her what had happened. "Mummy doesn't want me to play any more," she said, "because I'm not winning." '

Of course this isn't quite as extreme as the Frenchman who drugged his son's tennis opponents but who's to say to what depths some people plunge to ensure game, set and match? Charlene and her fiancé, Mark, were so convinced their eight-month-old son would become a successful athlete that they named him JJ because it sounds like a catchy sports name.

'Did you see the try I scored? Did you, sir?' crows a muddy but victorious boy to his coach, to be reminded there is no 'i' in 'team'. 'It never used to happen before,' observes the coach philosophically. 'Before it was team-work and no one took the glory but it's tougher on kids now. It's hard not to crow when you have your parents baying on the touchline.' Worst of all, though, is sports day because then everyone is there to watch and isn't there a lot to prove?

When once your mother came in a hat and sat on a folding stool with a flask of tea, now it's stopwatches and testosterone. In 2005 *Country Life* magazine, a study of twenty-five schools found that families no longer 'sit back, relax and enjoy the day'. Parents' races had been banned at seventeen institutions because the competitors were 'over-zealous', it said, and some parents were accused of 'spoiling' events by putting too much pressure on children to succeed. Pleasant egg-and-spoon and sack races have become a thing of the past. Says the then editor Clive Aslet: 'Nowadays, some parents have a highly competitive attitude to life and are neurotic about their children succeeding at everything they attempt.' Cheating was even reported to have gone on during some events. Now that's just not cricket.

In the arts, of course, the PP can appeal to teachers to allow our children the opportunity to show what we are so sure they are capable of. 'Choir school parents are the worst,' moans one teacher. ' "My child needs a solo," one mother insisted to me. "It's good for her self-esteem." '

The literature for the National Children's Orchestra asks parents (and children, to be fair) not to complain if they are in the second violins. The seconds, you are assured, play just as important a role in the orchestra. Second? Isn't second place the first loser?

School plays are a minefield of parental performance anxiety. How *can* they have cast Bettina as the third fairy from the left? She's the perfect lead. What are they thinking of? Marianne is an old hand at directing young talent. 'We have to be so careful what we choose for the school play. You have to find one that the whole year group can be in and there aren't many of those. We can't put on anything where there are only a few lead parts because it becomes so difficult with parents asking why their child hasn't been given the main character to play. We have to keep records of who had big parts in the past.'

Well, if he can't play Hamlet then you can make certain his costume will get him noticed. So you sit up till the wee hours sewing on bits of braid and lace, employing long-forgotten skills at chain stitch to ensure it's a work of art. That'll clinch it, you think, as you proudly send off the costume in a carrier bag, only to find that not only has everyone else hired theirs from a shop, one mother has had her son's costume sent up from a West End show.

'We had one girl with university don parents,' explains one teacher. 'If she went out to tea with a friend she had to make up the time with work later. We did a Greek play – Lord knows why now – and the mother went to each performance, never taking her eyes off the text to make sure her child was word perfect.'

So endemic is the PP, there is even support literature for the children of them. So why are we doing it? There has to be an element of 'I never did it so you can do it on my behalf' going on here. You didn't quite make the grade on the football field so you'll make sure your son is centre-half for Arsenal. But there has to be a big dollop of basking in their successes. If Tabitha gets the high jump cup or comes first in the 400m – well, just who created those legs, hey?

Dependent parents

'A new trend I have noticed,' says Margaret, 'is the needy parent, the one who can't make a decision for themselves without bringing it to me first. This isn't just about their child – I'm marriage guidance counsellor, family therapist, I've even been asked what they should do with the mother-in-law over Christmas.'

But isn't there something quite comforting about your children's teachers? With such paucity of sensible support from our elders about, a friendly face at the school gate, especially someone who takes our beloved children under their wing, takes us back to the days when we had teachers and they smelt nice. They tell you how wonderful your children are and you want to hug them and ask them, 'So am I doing it right?' They ought to know, after all.

' "Will damp come up through the buggy wheels?" is one of the more exceptional things I've been asked,' says Alice, who has thirty years' teaching under her belt. 'Though I did have one boy in my class whose mother latched on to me. She clearly did everything for him. He was very overweight and did nothing. He couldn't even dress himself for PE. Somehow she found out where I lived and she used to come over and ask me advice. One day she came to say she wanted to enter her son for a talent contest on TV and the researchers wanted to come to her house to discuss it. Could she borrow some of my furniture to tart her house up a bit?!'

Of course it's the older teachers we turn to. No point asking the young whippersnappers, is there? Not when, like policemen, they look younger and younger. Heavens, you barely trust them to be out of short pants themselves. Teaching has to be one profession where for once experience is respected. They've seen it all, wiped the bottom and worn the aertex blouse.

'I have to say, though, that I have never known a generation of parents that are so needy,' says Alice, 'and yet give in so easily to their children. It's as if everyone has a right to be happy and so do their children. Nothing must upset them.' Was this the rationale behind the father who rang her late one evening, beside himself with worry. 'I persuaded someone I met who knows you socially to give me your home number. I'm so sorry to call you but I am frantic.' It turned out his six-year-old daughter was sitting on the windowsill, legs dangling out, refusing to come in. Could Alice possibly come over and talk her down?

Teacher's presents

You've forged the homework, and forced the odd issue, but the end-of-term present is the opportunity to sink to outright bribery. Might something a little special ease the way? How can Mr Fellows fail to fast-track George if I give him two bottles of Châteauneuf-du-Pape for Christmas?

When we were kids you might go in with a bunch of flowers at the end of the summer term. A few sweet peas nicked from the garden taken in clasped in a sweaty hand was all it took, and a home-made card would earn you a kiss on the cheek.

Now teachers' gifts have reached unparalleled levels of competitiveness, and places like M&S and supermarkets are even offering boxes of chocolates and bath goodies wrapped specially with sugary messages. The whole issue is fraught with anxiety and uncertainty. A bottle of bath oil? Too obvious – they must have loads of the stuff. A voucher for the garden centre? Too impersonal. I know: an Armani scarf. That'll show how grateful you are.

Of course you have already contributed a tenner to the

class present, the purchase of which will be organised by some eager beaver who will hand round a card for you to sign and make a little speech as she hands over the garden bench she bought with the proceeds of the whip-round. (A tenner each for a class of thirty – you do the figures.) But, racked with uncertainty that the teacher won't truly acknowledge your contribution, you get a little something to hand over on the last day, *just in case*.

'It is great to have a real treat, but what I have a drawerful of is the home-made cards and letters from the children. That's what matters,' says one teacher.

Then the relief when they move on to secondary school and the whole thing fizzles out. But, help, you think, how can you influence things now?

One-Up-Parentship: what they say and what they mean

Isn't it exhausting running them from pillar to post?
(But when they are as talented as my children, it's a crime not to.)

It's so hard to find trousers to fit Tommy. They are always long enough on the leg but too big around the waist
(because he's so slim and athletic, unlike your porker).

I'm rushed off my feet
(because I have a job and you don't, you loser).

Lucky you, not having to freeze on the touchline.
(Oh, wasn't she picked for the team? Tough.)

Yes, I've heard the high school's very good now
(but I won't have to worry cos mine is bright enough to pass the eleven-plus).

Oh, I do envy you going to Cornwall *again*

  (because even though we are going club class it will still take us hours to get to Dubai).

You are so sensible not to buy a new buggy for each child

  (but I did because I can).

My children are so busy

  (cos I'm a great mother).

We don't fly long-haul any more, because of the carbon emissions.

  (We've hit hard times.)

You're lucky your daughter eats anything. Amelia is sooo picky

  (but that's because she has a highly refined palate).

He's just tired.

  (He's just not very good at it.)

Your daughter has a lively personality

  (and is a pain in the arse to teach).

Your daughter has a lively personality

  (which is a good thing because she's thick as a brick).

James has had the opportunity to learn to write his own prayers this term

  (but he didn't bother to take it).

Harriet contributes freely in class

  (in fact, she never bloody shuts up).

Your son does not accept authority easily.

  (Is his father in prison?)

Oscar is a solitary child.

  (Could he bath more often?)

6
Food: A War of Nutrition

It's five o'clock on a sunny evening. You have spent the last hour lovingly preparing organic carrots, butternut squash and puréed spinach for your family's dinner. You couldn't add chicken because that might be contaminated. It couldn't be beef because even now you're still a bit iffy about the BSE issue. It couldn't be lamb either because the butcher at the organic farm shop couldn't guarantee that it had been read a bedtime story every night before it was despatched to lamb heaven.

In fact it couldn't be meat at all because a vegetarian diet, so you have read, is far preferable, though you are carefully balancing iron and protein intake and macronutrients with organic free-range eggs and bioflavinoids – though not nuts because . . . well, you just never know, do you. Cheese of course is out because of your son's eczema and milk will only exacerbate his asthma and sinus problems.

Eventually, exhausted, with a glow of self-congratulation about you, you summon them to the table where you like to meet as a family to share news of your day and enjoy the shared pleasure of food together.

Ha! Dream on, sister. What you actually get is 'I'm not touching this' defiance, demands for ketchup or a flat refusal to try even the smallest bit of anything.

Let's face it, food is to being a modern parent what Al-Qaeda is to world security: an ever present terror. And just the mention of the subject can bring out a twitch in even the most level-headed, highly educated person. In fact you can forget education, the quality of what's on TV, the downfall of the civilised world. It's what goes into our children's stomachs that is the ultimate torment and it's like that before a nipple or a bottle (if you can live with yourself) even goes near their newborn mouth.

Ironic, isn't it, that at a time of concern about health, fast food and the time bomb of unparalleled obesity – a third of kids being seriously overweight in the UK according to the latest findings – we, whose children probably enjoy the best diet ever, obsess manically.

For Starters

From the moment a woman pees on the Stick and discovers she is up the duff, we have to question everything that goes in *our* mouths. Never mind that we are the generation who were gestating as our mothers smoked, drank gin and went to cocktail parties. Never mind that for thousands and thousands of years women have procreated successfully without having to read a magazine about what to eat while they are doing it. We dare not put more than 6oz of tuna in our mouths for fear of mercury levels; we find ourselves steering clear of Ardennes pâté and Brie. Potatoes can be dodgy – can't remember why now – and liver is a no-no. Dioxins and PCBs are everywhere, we hear, and, of course, up to the twelfth week we should have our 400 micrograms a day of folic acid.

If you are not in a state of complete nutritional confusion by now – your conscience being seriously pricked by the Twix you are demolishing that you have been craving all day – then take the weight off your varicose veins and take comfort in the fact that these are just the foothills of the massive ramifications the F-word will have in your life as a parent.

The Boob Job

Breast is best as we already know, and when the little mite is born there is the expectation that you will breastfeed. If you can manage it then the world applauds you – unless you try it in a pub – and you find yourself in the most bizarre places exposing a part of your anatomy you have only ever kept for your very nearest and dearest (and that time on St Tropez – well, everyone else was topless). The baby starts to suck and you have to hold tight to the other breast in case you shower the person sitting on the other side of the room, but you look down in glowing satisfaction as your baby suckles, knowing you are giving it the best you possibly can.

Unless of course you had a curry last night. Or oranges. Or a Pot Noodle. Or alcohol. Or a ready meal. So still we obsess about everything that goes in *our* mouths too. We know deep down that the quality of breast milk is only affected in extreme cases of deprivation and that the baby will take everything from you sooner than suffer itself, but still we worry that, unless we are careful, our children will not become the concert pianists they might be. We gobble up greedily the advice about staying clear of pollutants like nicotine and pesticide residue. We fret about insecticides (especially in airborne forms such as aerosols or coils) and seek out citronella. We fill our shopping trolleys with asparagus, cabbage, corn, chickpeas and spinach because we read somewhere that they contain lots of folic acid, and we search the net for foods with vitamin B9. It's the only vitamin that might just be slightly lacking in the diets of Western women so it's best to take a belt and braces approach, isn't it?

But, like the ability to do geometry or card tricks, some women can and some just can't breastfeed. 'I know I'd like to be doing it. I know I should be doing it. I know that formula milk is no substitute,' frets Belinda. 'There's even a political agenda: I know that there are issues about big corporations encouraging mothers in the Third World to feed their babies formula and I shouldn't be putting money in their pockets. So I pretend to everyone that I am – and the real reason I lie? Because I feel ashamed that I'm not doing the *best for my baby*.'

So what do we do? Sit and watch other women whip out their nipples at the drop of a breast pad as we fuss over bottles and warmers and microwaves (Should you? Shouldn't you? What about the hot spots?), trying hard to play down the faff involved. But take heart because even breastfeeding can have its pressures. Try to continue breastfeeding when you go back to work and you spend every waking hour frantically squeezing your boobs until

'You've got to hide those – I'm supposed
to be breastfeeding.'

they ache to produce enough milk for the au pair to give the baby during the day when you are out (and trying not to leak). That bottle in the fridge, waiting to be heated and served, contains all the guilt and all the best intentions in the world.

Ann even hired a pump so she could keep feeding Tom while she went back to her PR job. 'I just couldn't get on with those hand action things,' she says. 'They just didn't seem to fit my boobs but I couldn't bear not to express. One night at about midnight, feeling like a Holstein Friesian on this blasted pump thing, I realised that 3fl oz of breast milk was costing me about a quid!'

Alexis, determined she was going to take the bottle route for newborn James, came across the most bizarre double standard. 'There was the midwife sitting on my bed in the hospital telling me how I should be trying to breastfeed but I told her I didn't want to and that I found the whole thing disgusting. "So you are decided?" she asked finally. "Yup," says I. "Right, that's fine," she replied. "I couldn't stand it either. Stick to your guns, girl"!'

The Body Politic

So where did this war of nutrition come from? When did food become the enemy? The problem seems to be that the chasm between the classes has never been wider than it is today and never wider than it is about food. In the world that is eating worse junk than ever, where obesity is at epidemic proportions, where the first words for most children in the Western world are 'Happy Meal', and where even dinner ladies don't recognise a French bean, the classes-with-a-conscience are more terrorised by food than ever.

'I seem to compensate for the world's ignorance on my own children,' says Sarah, a usually sensible GP with a daughter of eleven and a son of eight. 'I'm manic about making sure they eat the five portions of fruit and veg a day and my children sigh and count them out. Deep down I know they should be having seven but I don't want to push the point.' What she forgets is that her kids have probably the best diet in the whole world even if they only had a couple of extra apples a week!

Food has become the enemy because, in most cases, food is the enemy. Our 'madness' about what we put in our children's mouths might just be justified when it is revealed there is more protein and less fat and salt in dog food than a fast food burger; that every month more than 90 per cent of the children in the United States eat at McDonald's, and a double quarter-pounder with cheese and medium fries is 1,110 calories and 1,330mg of sodium. Even the pap we are told about the value of low-fat foods becomes deeply suspicious when we find out McD's low-fat salad dressing has 730mg of sodium per 1.5 fl oz – and that's McDonalds' own nutritional information.

But let's not bang on about it (oh please, just one more: per ounce, Chicken McNuggets contain twice as much fat as a hamburger). We all know it's junk food and that only a fool would let their children eat it – you *don't*, do you? What's more scary and more likely to drive us to insane levels of eco food terror is that we are trying to raise children in a country where 40 per cent of the population have allergies of some kind – or at least they think they do. You can't take a step without hearing about asthma-related food intolerances, rashes and dermatitis, not to mention anaphylaxis. There is seafood allergy, rubber latex allergy, yeast, sesame and wheat. Milk, gluten and nickel too.

Supermarkets and food producers live in terror of mis-labelled packaging: Kettle sea salt and balsamic vinegar Chips were recently recalled as cheese seasoning had been mistakenly used instead of vinegar flavouring in two batches. Yikes. The implications.

A 'nut check' at a recent residential course for children turned out not to be a medical once-over to see if the wedding tackle was in order, or even a psychiatric assessment. It was so the matron could ensure no one had sneaked in sweets which the 'significant number of nut allergic children on the course might get hold of'.

Feeding Others

Allergies are not funny and, if you are affected, they can be deadly serious, but they are definitely not something our parents had to contend with. Lucy finds it makes a maniac of her: 'The whole thing about food and what you give other children is a minefield. I have been given an epi pen by the mother of a child who came to play and who had a nut allergy and I was absolutely demented. He was almost eating in a sealed area, because I thought, I've got peanut oil. If he inhales the vapours . . . and once upon a time that bowl had cashew nuts in it . . . The burden of responsibility was just unbelievable.'

And it doesn't stop there, does it? We have to take on responsibility elsewhere too, where perhaps others should. We can't relax in the knowledge that the powers that be are feeding our children properly. Once our school meals were made on the premises by a kindly crew of dinner ladies who peeled potatoes and made liver casserole and jam roly-poly and custard, which we'd go and run off afterwards with PE. Now the choice is turkey twizzlers and chips and chips and chips and there is no time for PE because the children have to do the literacy hour.

And it takes a TV celeb to take it in hand and make a political issue of what should be a nutritional one.

Food is political conflict too and everyone knows that in politics, there madness lies. We've already mentioned the formula milk issue but in your shopping trolley are bananas or a jar of coffee or carton of orange juice that aren't just lying there being bananas or jars of coffee or cartons of orange juice. They don't just make a comment about your choice of diet. They represent a war about Third World exploitation, price rigging and child labour that's going on way over your head and beyond Tescos on the South Circular. Crikey – shopping has never been such a drama.

Don't do what I do!

But don't you find yourself laying down one set of rules for yourself and one for your children? In our crusade to make sure that they have only the best of the best, we end up imposing really quite unreasonable limitations and even expectations on them. Claudia is aware she might be losing her sense of reason. 'Fast food joints are a bit of an issue for me, but I need to go there because otherwise my daughter will discover them and spend her entire life in fast food joints sitting over one of those full ashtrays and drinking bad coffee. The messages, though, are completely wrong. My children have to have chewy apricot bars which I wouldn't eat if I was starving.'

These look suitably disgusting and inedible, you think, as you put the cereal bars in your trolley for their school snacks then, at the checkout and feeling peckish, you slip in a bag of Minstrels for you for the journey home.

If it's not one thing . . .

But when you have finished the chocolate and secreted the wrapper, you can take comfort in the fact that never before have parents been bombarded with so much contradictory information. It's not really surprising that we are confused when we are surrounded by a media that is so keen on one hand to impart scary information about food and, on the other, to give us dogmatic advice about what we should and should not be eating

One minute omega 3 is the elixir of life. You see it everywhere – in special cartons of juice, eggs and spread. There are websites about it and you find yourself reading the back of packets and adding capsules of it to the vitamins and mineral supplements your children are already taking. Next thing you know, it's been decided it's not quite as essential as we'd first thought.

'I fell completely for the organic baby food thing,' says Fran, 'and paid well over the odds for the jars because if I was going to do jars then I had to do the organic jars. Then I read that I was better making non-organic home-made food. You can't win.'

You certainly can't. 'Not when supermarkets and food producers are packaging baby foods with the suggestion that they know best,' complains Jenny. 'One is doing quinoa, blueberry and spinach mushed up for babies. Oh, I found myself thinking, I hadn't thought of that. What is my child missing out on? I've never even heard of a bloody quinoa yet I found myself obsessing about it. I surfed the web in a panic about superfoods. What had I done? Millie was twenty-two months and she still hadn't had squash and sweet potato! What's even weirder is that I could so easily have made these foods myself and instead, like an automaton, I found myself buying them ready done!'

So while baby magazines and weekend sections in national newspapers ramp up the pressure, we seem to lose our ability to make informed decisions. We have very strong opinions as to whether the current government is good for the nation but we're stymied when it comes to something as complicated as butternut squash. Instead of using our common sense and cooking for ourselves, we find ourselves surfing chummy websites that are selling 280g of 'proper organic home-made' chicken in white sauce with sweetcorn and carrots for £3.20. Hang on a minute . . .

But don't just blame the media, poor lambs. Even the medics mess with our heads. Now we are told by the World Health Organisation that for the last forty years we have been given the wrong advice about breastfeeding and that weight charts used to advise us on a baby's optimum size have been based on the growth rates for infants fed on formula milk. There you were thinking you were doing the right thing, bucking the national trend and breastfeeding, only to be told your baby was underweight and you should supplement with a bottle or boost his solids. Aaaaargh!

But if only food was about eating

How many times have you heard yourself saying, 'When I was a little girl/boy I ate what was put in front of me and was grateful for it'? Food is a weapon even before it goes in the mouth, and the ones with their fingers on the trigger? The children.

It was all so easy before. You'd invite friends over for dinner and they'd be full of praise about your ceviche, go away asking for the recipe and all would be lovely. Now for your beloved child, the reason for your existence, you do the same. Not quite a Nigella recipe but as much an offer of love (because as we all know, food is love), and you get complete and utter rejection. Nobody warned us, did they? No one said that the subject of mashed carrots and swede would reduce you to tears. There was a conspiracy of silence about the fact that you could sweat for hours over shepherd's pie or chicken and mash only to find yourself faced with a closed mouth. In fact there is a direct connection between the amount of time you spend making it and the likelihood of rejection.

We have control everywhere else, haven't we? We can make them wear a jumper, we can do our best to get them to bed at night, we can decide where they are going to school, but one broccoli floret and we have met the intractable because food is a lethal weapon in the arsenal of the under-eighteens.

And doesn't the rejection make you psychotic? 'I would hold open his mouth and force-feed him like those poor geese in the Périgord,' confesses Kate. 'I had slaved over the stuff and even though he's only two and a half, he somehow *knew*. He was like Damien in that horror film. I felt he had total control and there was nothing I could do.'

'I'd get it in her mouth,' says Maggie, mum to Natasha, 'but then she'd sit like a hamster with it stored in her cheeks. I tried every trick in the book – diversion, bribery, anger – and she'd chew and chew until it was unswallow-able, then I'd watch as she spat out everything on to the plate.'

The pleasure we feel as we watch a child swallow a forkful of vegetables is second only to winning the Nobel Peace Prize in terms of achievement, so in that blob of masticated dinner, regurgitated on to the plate, lies our failure as a parent.

But isn't food supposed to be about pleasure? Isn't it supposed to be an enjoyable experience – I mean, what are restaurants all about otherwise? Why was the Michelin star invented if it was about misery and suffering? Well,

'Can I have some guacamole with that?'

yes, it is supposed to be, but when it comes to children, food is a symbol of all we are trying to achieve. We want to give them good things in a world of bad ones, and they'd sooner have a burger and chips.

Compromise . . . yours!

So what do you find yourself doing? Bending over backwards to keep everyone happy so long as they eat the stuff, and preparing about as many meals as the Ivy on a busy night. Potatoes are prepared in all manner of ways – one won't eat boiled, the other prefers mash – and chicken is being grilled because the tuna bake you so lovingly prepared is simply not acceptable. Mind you, a mother who offers fish in any form is either brave or downright foolish (okay, so yours *love* it. Don't get smug).

Then you read the food pages of parenting magazines. 'Here's a recipe for coconut cakes that are a simple, scrumptious treat that kids and parents can make together.' Oh, crikey, you think, not only have you not made those, you didn't make it a bonding experience by doing it *with your child*.

The Stasi of control, though, is the faddy eater. Now to some children this might just be some emotional response to food and they will probably grow up obsessive compulsive and unable to leave the house without checking three times they've turned off the gas. But to most, refusing to eat anything but Barbie tinned pasta and Monster Munches is downright dictatorial. In fact it makes Stalin look soft. What kind of glee must these faddists experience as they watch us plead, beg, weep until we cave in and heat up a tin. Anything, anything to get the little sod to eat.

What's even more bizarre is good food becomes bad and bad food, good. Claudia sums it up: 'We get the organic box, we go to the organic market, we have risotto. They have all the posh organic stuff they could possibly eat but when they are having a treat, it's tack – it's horrible, pink, sugary, marshmallow, chocolatey horror.' The message seems to be this: Be good and you will be given a reprieve from this healthy diet. You will be allowed to eat sweet rubbish that tastes nice.

Out to lunch

There's another mistake we are making too and that's confusing taking children to a restaurant with a treat. Get it right: restaurants are a treat for *adults*. They are a break from cooking; a place to have a few glasses of wine and a chat with friends; a place to go on a date or for a gourmet experience. To children, if they don't sell chips and large ice cream sundaes, they are pointless. Burger King calls itself a restaurant. So does Le Gavroche. So why doesn't the latter serve ketchup?

When will we ever learn? Gizelle has 'almost given up going out to restaurants now because it is just too difficult to eat with your child. I mean, by the time they have drunk the milkshake you bought them to keep them quiet before the food arrives, they are full and you're like, "Well, wouldn't you like your goujons of fish?" And you end up eating them because you don't want to let it go to waste.'

'When we were kids it was such a big treat – prawn cocktail and a steak at a restaurant the night before we went back to school,' remembers Gill. 'Now we meet friends at lunchtime and we all think, Won't this be nice? All of us out with the kids having a bite to eat. But in fact I always come away vowing I'm never, ever doing that again. The kids get restless and start getting up and throwing chips at each other or bits of torn-up napkin, and you are trying to listen to keep up with the adult conversation with half an eye on the people frowning at you from tables close by.'

For some bizarre reason, we think going out to a restaurant with children is some form of hospitality. A happy get-together. Actually it's a nightmare of stamina and tolerance. Like everything else they want it here and they want it now. It is beyond them that they might have to wait, and you know what's mad? We don't insist they learn how to. 'I have a bag full of tricks,' says Ann-Marie with a laugh, who finds herself out too often with Will, eight, and Charlotte, six. 'Everything in my head is telling me this is bloody stupid and we should have stayed at home, so, like Mary Poppins, I have a bag full of diver-sionary toys – crayons, Gameboys, you name it – instead of just telling them to be patient. What on earth am I afraid of?'

Ha! Now that's the million-dollar question.

'Oh, but he simply adores squid ink pasta . . .'

We have been programmed since we were cooking roast mammoth risotto over the cave fire that it is good parenting to nourish. If you feed your children well, then you are a *good parent*. And when it gets scary is when your skills are revealed for everyone else to judge.

It's a bit like giving a dinner party and getting into a complete panic that the food won't be good enough. Only a hundred times worse. Never mind that most of the population are popping take-away chips into their offspring's mouths in the pram. It doesn't even matter that to the majority of the population a microwave beefburger will suffice as nutrition. *What will other people think* if your children are seen to be eating a bag of crisps?

'We went to the planetarium on a school trip,' says Lucy, fretting about the whole issue. 'The hardest part of the day was lunch because everybody just sat down and got out their lunchboxes, and the parents were saying: "He's got Cheese Strings! Have you seen he's got Cheese Strings?" And the effort that other people had put into their lunchboxes that day knowing that other people were going to be looking was phenomenal. Everything has to be organic and free-range this and good for you and healthy that.' So terrified was she that, even at school, she would be judged by lunchbox, Lucy found herself putting together a five-course meal for her son's lunchbox. 'I realised that perhaps I was going a bit far when I peeled a quail's egg. I thought, Hang on, this is just like Henry VIII's banquet here. And he's five.'

Her paranoia is entirely justified. There's an insufferable modern smugness between parents, which didn't exist before the invention of the organic rice cracker. Admit it, doesn't it give you a teensy-weensy bit of satisfaction when your children say, 'Can I have an apple?' or 'Oh, I do love tapenade,' in front of other people? Ann has a theory: 'We like to sort of present ourselves and we can do that through food, can't we? We can show who we are through what we give our kids and what we give their kids, but we need to make sure everybody knows. When we are having kids over, sometimes I get to the stage where I'm almost throwing a mini dinner party and they're six! It has got ridiculous.'

'If I provide sausages to a child who comes over to play,' admits Pru, 'I do worry what the other parents will think.'

There's a sweet satisfaction, isn't there, though, when the mother comes to collect the playmate and you say, 'Oh, he ate *really* well. He even had seconds of baby corn/ cottage pie/foie gras,' and you watch the delicious terror in her eyes as she says, 'He never eats that at home.' Ha, you find yourself thinking, isn't it lucky then that your child has had the privilege of lunch with us! You turn into this hateful person who says things like, 'Oh, I only ever buy from the farmers' market,' or, 'George is always nagging me to make my pasta puttanesca.' We don't talk like this in other areas of our life, so why on earth are we doing it here?

Of course there is the odd mad one. The parent who swoops on your house and does a food standards report on your larder. One woman, whose child shows no allergies whatsoever, is so traumatised by the thought of them, that she insists nothing potentially allergenic is served at parties *her* son attends.

There's an odd sort of reversal here, though, with this food thing. There are the type of parents who try to be so laid back. 'Oh, yes,' they say languidly, 'we don't mind Jocasta having a bag of Hula Hoops.' Yet you know behind closed doors it's a different story. 'I go out of my way to make it known that my kids are allowed chocolate,' says Liz, 'but in fact that's not true at all. I'm really really careful not to let them have junk, but where I live it's not seen to be cool to be super organic and good and healthy because we are all quite geeky so we pretend to be cool!'

Your children come back from a day of ice cream and Coke with the grandparents and you find yourself contemplating colonic irrigation for them to purge them of this muck. Think what it will do to their well-being and intelligence!

Out of the mouths of babes

Scarier though than our own obsessions, scarier than the disapprobation of other parents is judgement by children themselves.

Part of the curriculum seems to be Keep Your Parents in Order. Clare recently bought some organic strawberries grown in some sunny clime for a special treat for her twins in January. 'Look!' she yelped in glee, bringing them out at the end of the meal as a surprise, only to be met by stony silence. The twins exchanged glances. 'Mum, they've been flown here.' 'So?' 'Well, that uses up fossil fuels and that's contributing to global warming.'

So when did food get so wrapped up in everything: rejection of love, control, the downfall of the planet? It's like living with Friends of the Earth.

'My poor child is like a neurotic Woody Allen figure who paces around the kitchen obsessing about whether or not he has had his five portions of fruit and veg that day,' says Lucy. 'And he's so Mc-phobic that every time we drive past McDonald's he is jeering at people; and food's all colour co-ordinated now. You have to have a piece of red food, blue food, yellow food and it gets to the point where he is saying, "Oh, but Mummy I've had lots of red food today, I should be having blue food," and you are going through the cupboards trying to find a blueberry or a prune or something so you can tick it off the list.'

It's that gastro-terrorism again, only now they aren't refusing to eat the good food that you have so lovingly prepared. They are criticising you for not being good enough. At worst, it's horrendous – and ends up with eating disorders and self-loathing. At best it's distressing, but you know they'll get their comeuppance when they have kids themselves. Then we'll get the last laugh.

Until then we cave in. 'It's been more than a year since I've been allowed to consume the froth on my cappuccino,' coos some self-satisfied food writer. 'Screams of rage ensue if my two-year-old is not allowed to skim it all off with a spoon.' Oh, fear not: market forces will out. Costa and Starbucks now do a Babyccino so the little darlings can have their own way.

You've cooked up a little foodie if your child:
- Thinks McDonald's is a farm
- Gives Smarties back to you because she thinks they're counters
- Uses the Playdoh machine to make pretend fresh pasta
- Looks at a picture of a fish finger and has no idea what it is
- Plays pretend games about eating imaginary 'couscous'
- Tries white chocolate for the first time and says, 'This Brie is very nice'
- Wants a juicer for his birthday
- Asks at the chip shop if they have balsamic vinegar
- Goes on a school trip to France and brings you back a Fourme d'Ambert as a souvenir
- Thinks Pizza Express is fast food

7
Family Holidays: Travelling Hopefully

Remember holidays before we had children? Remember relaxing, winding down, doing what we felt like doing? Returning home tanned, restored and revitalised? Well, we can forget all that, because none of it applies any more, once we start going on holiday with kids. And a week in a caravan at Camber Sands, knocking about with a bucket and spade, won't cut the mustard any more.

In fact, what it really needs these days is a new name – one that has no association with relaxation or pleasure – to describe going through the same shit in a new place with none of the customary support around, tacking on an arduous long-haul journey at both ends, and the privilege of paying through the nose for it, cos we're going in the school holidays.

Face facts. Holidays are no holiday, but since we persist in pretending they are, we have to play the game and all convince each other (and maybe ourselves) that we're actually enjoying our two weeks in the sun. Whereas the truth is that we generally can't wait to go back home. It rapidly becomes clear that what we and our children want from a holiday is completely incompatible – like matter and antimatter. If we are having a good time, they'll be whining. If they are enjoying themselves, we'll be counting the seconds until it's over. And this is something that will go on until the day we can go our separate ways.

The Expense!

Do you too get a sense of panic as term draws to a close? How could they do that to us? Leave us on our own with all those children to look after? And the expense! Because, let's face it, school holidays are expensive now – and that's even before we go anywhere. If we're working, there's childcare. If we're not, we've got to take them places. When we were kids, we'd cycle up to the sweet shop, go and dig holes on the golf course, climb trees and practise whistling, then hiding when somebody looked around. Ah, happy days! Now, kids out on their own are targets of suspicion and resentment, and run the risk of getting ASBOs for not tucking their shirts in or breathing too loudly. So we have to keep them gainfully employed at all times. And that costs.

Lisa fumes, 'We've got to take them places in the car, feed them – cos they want feeding all the time – take them to the cinema, theme parks, day trips, swimming. If we can find somewhere for them to let off some energy on a sports course, we'll pay through the nose. And on top of all that, they'll need extra credit on their phones so they can text each other about what a boring time they're having! It's six weeks of me not being able to do anything I want to do. And when I said that to my daughter one time, she said, "Well, now you know how I feel when you make me go to school." As if it was a choice!'

Despite all the money and time we're throwing at our kids, 24 per cent of parents expect their children will complain of being bored at least once a week during the holidays. Only 24 per cent? These people are not doing right by their kids! If we deny our children the pleasure of whining, 'You're totally ruining my life!' at regular intervals then we are depriving them of a right we all enjoyed as kids. Come on, slackers! Toughen up! Take some pride in your role as parents!

Planes, trains and automobiles

Of course, the first problem with holidays is that we have to get there and, whatever mode of transport we choose, we're going to suffer. A survey commissioned by the games-maker Ravensburger reveals that children squabbling is the biggest cause of holiday stress. No shit, Sherlock! Well, no doubt a bracing game of draughts would sort that out. Or maybe soundproof glass between the front and back seats of the car. Now why don't the manufacturers think of these things? Why don't they ever ask us?

Cram our family into a little tin box for hours on end, and we're bound to have trouble. Particularly when the very first, 'Are we nearly there yet?' generally comes about eight miles from home.

Ginny shakes her head in disbelief. 'Despite the fact that the kids get really car sick, we decided to drive to the south of France. How crazy is that? We had a car full of wet wipes, bottled water and empty carrier bags and we just went for it. It became some sort of twisted macho compulsion to see how many miles we could cover without stopping. And when we got back, that was virtually all we talked about to other parents – how many miles we covered between stops.'

So if driving is hell, we take to the air. Or not. Next time someone tells you their kids will 'probably sleep through most of their transatlantic flight', just do them a favour and slap them hard at once. They need to be brought to their senses. Long-haul flights may be tedious for adults but for kids they're fantastically exciting. What could be better: strapped into a nice bouncy seat, with a tray to open and slam shut repeatedly, captive adults to pull faces at, regular if inedible food with sachets of salt and pepper to shake over everyone, then the promise of portable games consoles and in-flight movies if they get too restless. What possible reason could they have for sleeping?

Flying – progress? We've made ourselves victims of our own success by being able to access the whole world on a whim and a 747. Travel had to be easier when you were restricted to a week in Skegness.

Steve shakes his head at the memory. 'The kids made themselves sleep in the car to make sure they'd be awake for the whole ten hours. We were completely zonked after the long drive to the airport and in no mood for quality time with the little sods, but we had to take it in turns to stay awake with them to make sure they didn't drive everyone else on the plane crazy. I counted up the number of times they each went to the loo during my watch. Twenty-five.'

'Are we enjoying ourselves yet?'

We get into a particular grimly determined mindset when we're travelling with kids, and it's nothing to do with enjoyment or leisure. When we've got everything booked, it becomes an imperative to make it all go according to plan, despite misadventures. Defeat is simply not an option – particularly when we've saved up our air miles and everything is 'non-transferable'.

Roger shudders as he remembers the worst twenty-six hours of his life, travelling with his wife and eighteen-month-old daughter from Auckland to Fresno via Los Angeles by plane and rental car – all pre-booked. 'Little Julia had a gippy tummy in New Zealand and if we'd been even a tiny bit sane, we'd have stayed put. But all we could think about was the tickets, the reservations. It was hideous. She vomited all over us, then diarrhoea would leak out of her nappy. We'd change that and then she'd vomit again. We left the flight with a quarantine bag stuffed with soiled clothes – ours and Julia's. The flight staff even had to replace the seat cushions mid-flight because they were too awful to be used any more. Everyone must have hated us, but we were too stressed out even to notice.'

And baby came too

Travelling light is simply not an option any more. Because, obviously, if our baby doesn't have everything just the same as at home, he's going to be traumatised for the rest of his life. So in goes the nightlight (and an adaptor plug), in goes the musical cot mobile with the fluffy bunnies, in goes the cot bumper. And your case is full already. And then there's food.

Jenny remembers her first family holiday. 'As we all know, they don't have babies in Greece. So we decided we'd better take all Safia's food with us, just like at home. Because if we didn't, she'd cry, she wouldn't sleep, it would be a disaster. So we bought fifteen jars of her favourite banana mush. It weighed a ton, but we couldn't risk her eating foreign bananas – no, she had to have British bananas. And so I ended up taking almost no clothes. And all we took were nappies, factor squillion sun block and banana mush. Some holiday!'

Shared holiday, shared misery

Why is it that, when we've got kids, we suddenly think it would be a good idea to spend two weeks cooped up with another family, just because they've got kids too? What kind of madness is it that makes us think it's going to be somehow easier? Holidays are stressful enough as it is, with the whole dynamic of suddenly having to spend all day every day with your partner and your children; it's like a great big long weekend – and we all know how hellish those are. Add another family, going through the same agony and do it in a house with paper-thin walls and terrible plumbing, and Alcatraz would have been more of a laugh. At least there you had the option of being put in Solitary. Really, it couldn't be less relaxing, because we feel constantly on show so we're trying our hardest to present our family at its best and the whole thing turns into a competition.

Laura recalls, 'We thought we were the best of mates and the kids always got on so well. Now I realise it was only because we all had our own homes to go to, and we never had to have *breakfast together*. From the first morning, when their kids had croissants from the local boulangerie and our two wanted Shreddies, I knew we were in for trouble. The other dad kept laughing and saying our kids were wimps, in a really sneery way. I remember trying to force my daughter to eat this really garlicky pâté, just to show him. It ended up with an ugly showdown over some bouillabaisse.'

There were some upsides to Laura's holiday, though. 'The best thing was that our kids were much better swimmers than theirs and, since we had a pool at the villa, it was blatantly obvious. So to make up ground, my husband was nudging the kids, whispering, "Go on, do another length and a tumble turn, go on. I'll pay you!" It brought out the worst in us all. We've barely seen the other family since.'

Long-haul competition

The very best bit of the holiday, of course, is when we're back at home, all the misery behind us, and we give our (carefully revised) version of events to our friends. There's a definite hierarchy of holiday destinations but it's not all that obvious to the unwary. As time goes by, you'll catch on, but you'll have several years of polishing your anecdotes and buffing your tan, only to be trumped by a more experienced holiday boaster, before you get it quite right.

It's important to be detailed, of course. There is no point in saying, 'Oh, we went to Provence,' because any fool can do that. We have to find a hitherto barely known region of France or, alternatively, have a 'little place' there. If we can't manage that, a villa with a pool and preferably a cleaner is bound to wipe the smile off a few people's faces. And so it goes on, with the ante being upped and upped until we're spending the equivalent of the GDP of a small Eastern European country to take our kids to the Caribbean for island-hopping by private plane in the high season. Then, just when we think it can't be bettered, we'll meet someone who completely takes the wind out of our sails.

'I was so pleased with our holiday,' says Melanie. 'Well, smug would be more accurate. I was telling a woman who has a boy in the class above my son's. She listened politely and nodded but I know something was up. Then, when I'd finished going on about how brilliant Madagascar was, she just said, "We try not to fly long-haul any more. The damage to the environment is just so awful, isn't it? We just went to the Outer Hebrides for three weeks, in the most heavenly cottage with its own beach. We all just swam and sailed and canoed and windsurfed all day long, and the weather was perfect. We caught our own fish most days and cooked them on an open fire." And that was it. I was completely deflated. It had been *Swallows and Amazons*, she'd spared the environment *and* they'd saved money.'

See the genius of that woman? 'We try not to fly long-haul any more.' She not only has the moral high ground now, but she was taking her kids to exotic climes before we even thought about it. You have to admire a put-down like that.

Another useful ploy is to downplay our current holiday, along the lines of, 'We're just camping this summer. A couple of weeks in Cornwall,' then, when the person we're talking to has relaxed and admitted they're only going to poxy Normandy, we hit them with, 'because Whistler in spring is so expensive.' Game, set and match to us!

Ticking the boxes

If we really want to rate in the holiday game, we'll have to cover all bases: culture, adrenalin, something apparently unpretentious, luxury and something no one has thought of doing at all. And we must book it all up at least a year in advance, so we've got plenty of time to tell everyone: Easter in Seville, half-term on a sailing course in Antigua, summer hols in the Scillies, October in Mauritius, and the following February on a camel-riding course in Marrakech. Just think of the round robin we'll be able to make out of *that* next Christmas!

Children, of course, are mostly unaware of the relative costs of holidays and what they represent. Lucy was horrified when her kids came home from school on the first day of the autumn term: 'We'd been flotilla sailing in Croatia, then we spent a week on a gorgeous island. It really had been a fantastic holiday but, when the children got home from school that day, they kept going on and on

'That's not how you spell Mustique.'

about some kid in their class who'd been to Blackpool, and how much fun it sounded, and could we go there next year. Over my cold, lifeless body!'

The pressure works both ways, of course, with children asking to go to Mexico, like their friends, as if the decision were as simple as choosing a pizza topping. Often this is just due to lack of geographical knowledge. One seven-year-old said, 'Josh got his new football boots in South Korea.' And when his mother had picked herself up off the floor, he corrected himself, 'I mean South Kensington.'

A head teacher sighs, 'We had to put an end to holiday diaries because the differences in what the children had done over the summer were so huge. And we couldn't help thinking the parents were using the diary as a showcase for how fantastic they were. There were business-class plane tickets stuck in, pressed exotic flowers from Caribbean islands, photos of the villas they'd stayed in. And then we'd have the other extreme, with bus tickets and stories about going to the leisure centre for a swim.'

As long as it's educational . . .

So if children are at school for roughly thirty-nine weeks a year, that leaves just thirteen weeks for all these holidays. And don't the tour operators know it! Despite the efforts of the government, holiday prices zip up and up in the high season – it's simply supply and demand. No wonder parents want to take the kids on holiday during the school term – it's cheaper and quieter. Yes, but . . . er, what about their education?

Now that the DfES has come out so strongly against holidays in term time, we have to be able to justify going in terms of something other than a cost-saving exercise. So off we go, cap in hand to the head teacher, begging for our ten days out of the academic year, or even more if we can swing it. And it's entirely at the school's discretion – another reason to suck up to the head. If the head teacher won't agree, and we've booked the holiday already, we're in trouble. Our children will be considered to be truant-ing, just as surely as if we were letting them roam the streets sniffing glue, and, under the recent anti-social behaviour legislation, we could have to pay a fixed pen-alty. The shame of it!

Luckily for us, there are now plenty of holiday com-panies around who understand our needs. In recent years, the trend for more adventurous family holidays has really taken off, and we can always find a way of justifying these as 'educational', particularly when the tour operator throws in a bit of trekking and some ancient ruins. For example, on one tour we can travel down the Nile on a felucca, take in the Great Pyramid, a museum or two and find time for a little snorkelling in the Red Sea – all in the cosy company of like-minded, right-on people with chil-dren just like ours (we hope).

'After a day whale-watching in the bay of Algeciras, we had all gone up to a nature reserve in the hills of Andalucía to see vultures in their natural habitat. The parents were all being terribly right-on and taking photos, but the kids found some bones the vultures had stripped bare – apparently the farmers leave carcasses out for them. It was like something from *Lord of the Flies*! The kids made a huge pile of bones with skulls on top all facing outwards, then started leaping around with these horns held to their heads. They were all doing it, and all the parents looked terribly uncomfortable and embarrassed, but they didn't really want to bust it all up. In the end, one of the children tripped over and cut his knee and the whole thing ended. But it was a strange moment. I can't imagine what the tour guide must have thought.'

Think of the holiday diary we could have turned in after a trip like that! Trouble is we know the educational credentials of the 'adventure holiday' are bogus and a feeble excuse just to save on our holiday budget, but doesn't it make it so much easier when we go grovelling to the head? We can even take the brochure to prove its relevance to Key Stage whatever (printed on recyclable paper, natch).

Result? Happy head teacher and happy parents. And we can bet ours will be the only kids in the school to have done Costa Rica by the age of seven. Trouble is, they'd still probably prefer Blackpool.

Souvenirs that last and last

So why are we travelling to more and more far-flung regions with our children? Well, you can't expect rugged individualists of the Lonely Planet and Rough Guide generation to make do with a couple of weeks on the

Costa Brava once we have kids of our own, can you? We take long-haul travel so much for granted – indeed, it is usually a major strategy for defining ourselves as 'interesting' – that we would sooner fit the kids into our holiday plans than fit our holiday plan to the kids. The more unusual the destination, the better.

Yet with more exotic holidays come more exotic diseases. Travel clinics are reporting significant increases in the number of children being brought in for a full armful of inoculations. A nurse specialising in the field says, 'My nightmare client would be a pregnant woman with toddlers turning up and saying, "Oh, we're off to the Gambia the day after tomorrow. Can we have our jabs now?" If they took as much time looking into the health risks as they do trying to shave a few pounds off the price of their holiday, they'd be far better prepared. And there must be people who don't bother to see the doctor at all – until they come back from their holiday with amoebic dysentery or worse. And it's all so they can show off to their neighbours about the holiday they've had.'

Amoebic dysentery! What fun! A quick flick through one of the many brochures reveals a trip to Peru, recommended as suitable for children from the age of seven. And the health notes are as follows:

Disease	Vaccination
Diphtheria	Recommended
Malaria	Recommended**
Poliomyelitis	Recommended
Rabies	Recommended

Typhoid	Recommended
Yellow Fever	Compulsory*

*A Yellow Fever vaccination is highly recommended, even if arriving within 6 days from or via an infected area.

**Malaria: At time of writing there have been reports that a strain resistant to choloquine and sulfadoxine pyrimethamine has been identified.

Wouldn't that be enough to scare off the bravest? The idea of having those jabs as an adult, quite apart from having to drag a seven-year-old to the travel clinic to have them would end all holiday spirit in most families. Dr Lisa Ford, a lecturer in travel medicine, says, 'I would not take my young children to chloroquine-resistant malarious areas. I am very keen for them to experience the world soon, but for the time being what's wrong with Northumberland?'

Quite.

Everybody happy?

We know, don't we, that we can't please all the people all of the time. So why don't we stop trying? Taking teenagers on holiday – or in fact anywhere – is nightmarish at the best of times. But when we have to combine their interests with those of our younger children, let alone ours, we know we're heading for trouble. Time was teenagers just had to lump it and sulk for the statutory two weeks until they were old enough for an Interrail card and a backpack. Now their expectations are altogether higher.

The problem is that we would run a mile, clutching our ears, from the kind of resort they would enjoy and, equally, just the sight of a cathedral or (God forbid) a glass-blowing works sends them into a catatonic state that nothing but Bacardi Breezers, trip-hop and scantily clad members of the opposite sex will rouse them from.

Mandy remembers, with a shudder, their last family holiday. 'We'd hired a villa in Umbria and it cost an arm and a leg. The little ones were perfectly happy splashing about in the pool but my fourteen-year-old was furious with us for dragging her out there. She stayed in bed until lunchtime every day, and when she did get up, she complained constantly. She spent every night in her room playing music on her iPod. We'd have done better leaving her at home. Fortunately she stayed out of all the photos, so we didn't have to explain why we appeared to have a member of the Addams family with us. She went back paler than when she arrived. But when we got back, we still pretended we'd all had the jolliest time. Well, you've got to, haven't you?'

The final solution: holidaying together but apart

What's the point in flying halfway across the world to unwind in the lap of luxury if we have to spend our precious leisure time entertaining our own children? Where's the fun in that? If the worst part about the family holiday is the family part of it, then the solution is clear. Split up when you reach your destination and see as little of each other as you can until the flight home. Yes, this is the Kids' Club but five-star! And now parents have discovered how fantastic it is barely to see their kids at all during their holidays, clubs are springing up at luxury resorts everywhere. It's Butlins with palm trees.

Cathy sighs as she remembers her perfect holiday: 'I knew I was in heaven when a uniformed flunky from the hotel approached my sun lounger with a little cloth and a bottle of spray, offering to polish my sunglasses. And what was more, there were no shrieking children, no babies wailing, no sandy footballs landing on my tummy. It was almost spooky. All the kids were occupied for most of the day. I even started to miss mine but not all the parents were like me. We could see the strain for the hour or so they had to spend together each day. But that's what we pay for – someone else to keep our kids out of our way!'

But when children are welcome as long as they're somewhere else, what happens if we actually want to spend time with them? Come on! It could happen! 'I realised we weren't the typical clientele,' she continues, 'because we actually quite wanted to do things with our kids, but bringing them to the beach with us was very uncomfortable because they were just about the only children there. All the others were in the clubs, and there was plenty of tutting and eye-rolling going on when our two started to play ball in among the sun loungers. After that, we consigned them to the clubs, like everyone else.'

Closer to home, there's a burgeoning market for hotels that are child-friendly but we're not talking three-star properties in Bournemouth. These are the height of luxury, offering relaxation for stressed-out mummies and daddies so there's usually a spa attached. But also tagged on is a nursery (all Ofsted checked, of course) where their little darlings can be entertained morning till night (and out of sight), and you don't have any nasty feelings of guilt spoiling your hot stone massage. It's the best of both worlds – for the parents at least.

A Child's Right to Ski

Remember when a week on the piste was fancy? The preserve of royals and glamorous weather-beaten foreigners in fur hats? Those were the good old days, weren't they? When we could get away with not taking a skiing holiday every year, without permanently compromising our family's honour. Now, if we don't book into the Trois Vallées at February half-term, along with the majority of Western Europe, our kids are likely to place a call to ChildLine.

Harry wrings his hands, a shadow of the man he once was. 'I hate skiing,' he moans. 'But the kids insist so we have to. I'm terrified, broke and knackered from the moment we get to wherever we select each year. It's crowded, we have to queue with French people for goodness sake, it's noisy, it's cold, everything costs a fortune. There's always a chance of permanent disablement and, wherever we go, the snow's always better somewhere else. But the kids have to go, so I have to put up with it.'

Part of the problem, according to a ski instructor, is that no one will admit to being a beginner so they're always trying runs that are, frankly, too difficult for them.

Jenny remembers a late afternoon run when her nine-year-old daughter came with her. 'She'd been in ski school all week and I thought she was probably doing all right. My friend's daughter was quite good and I wanted Becky to keep up, so we all went together. It started out as a blue run, then there was a bit of red, then we were going to finish on a blue near the hotel. Well, I don't know what happened. We must have missed the sign for the blue and we ended up on a black. There was no way Becky could manage it and I could see she was starting to panic. I wasn't doing too great either. Then these stewards appeared with a sledge they use to pick up all the rubbish at the end of the day. They gave me such a look, as if I was the worst mother in the world, and took Becky down on the sledge. Thank goodness I don't speak French too well. I heard some people talking about it in the queue for the ski-lift the next day and I had to pretend it wasn't us.'

But even if we love skiing – and plenty of us do – there is one unpalatable truth we all have to understand. Tim puts it succinctly: 'I've just had to accept that my kids are far better at skiing than I will ever be. Now, they just regard me as an embarrassment. Basically, I'm the wallet and that's all I'm here for and as long as I keep providing the money but stay far enough away that they can disown me, we'll all have a good time.'

Latch-key effect

So are we any better off for the world being a global village? Isn't there something awfully wrong with our children not knowing where Yorkshire is while being totally au fait with the Yucatan Peninsula?

But you must have noticed how delighted your kids are when they get back home. What is it? The telly? The computer? The cat? No, in most cases, it's the plumbing. Sharon has noticed it too. 'We got in, unloaded the car and the kids were nowhere to be seen. We thought they'd slipped out without our noticing. Then we found each of them had locked themselves in the loos, one upstairs and one downstairs. When we asked them why – cos there was no sound of flushing or anything – they both said, "We just wanted to be alone for a bit." And, do you know, I knew how they felt.'

Why you need to be mad to have children . . .

	Then	**Now**
Average income	1970: £1,400 pa	£27,000
House prices (average)	1970: £4,480	£178,992
Week in a hotel in Cornwall for a family of four in summer	1972: £98 for seven nights	£3,080 for seven nights
Family estate car	1975: Austin Allegro 1500: £1,500	VW Touareg from £28,600
Fridge	1975: £79	£900
Pair of school shoes	1975: £5.50	£40
Pocket money (weekly)	5p	£7.24 average for 11–14-year-olds
Boarding school fees	1970: £640 per year	£20,000 (plus) per year
Pop music	1975: vinyl album £2	CD £13.99
Comics and magazines	1975: *Beano* 4p per week	*Warhammer* magazine £4 per month
Sweets	1975: Creme Egg 6p	Creme Egg 36p

Sources: Clarks Shoes, Nationwide, Halifax, Norland, *The Lady*, Nannypaye.co.uk, DC Thomson

8
Slaves to the Schedule

You've occupied them for the statutory vacation period by trekking in Nepal; now what are you going to do to fill up the rest of their spare time?

Activity 24/7 is a disease that seems to affect us modern parents. Like doing Sudoku, it becomes a compulsion. And there is less time left unused. Shooting the breeze is not an option. Boredom? Utterly verboten. Imagine the dangers in leaving them to fill their own time! It's no coincidence that the number of children who end up in A&E with injuries from home-made bows and arrows has taken a noticeable dip. And when was the last time you heard about someone falling out of a tree (excluding Keith Richards of course)? They've all been cut down anyway in case they grow conkers. When we were kids we could spend hours with just a stick and our imagination. Now our kids will get repetitive strain injury from opening the car door.

This need to account for every waking moment is partly a result of the same anxiety that stops them being allowed to do skipping in the playground: the perception of danger. We can't let them play in the woods after school or during the holidays, or go over to the village shop (if there still is one) because they will undoubtedly be run over, kidnapped or abducted by aliens, when in fact children are statistically safer now than they have ever been. The bigger danger they face is from having over-developed thumbs from texting or over-use of the game console.

Another reason we can't let our children just fill their time with nothing in particular is because we wouldn't really know what to do with them. 'I get quite incensed if they are watching TV,' admits Lily, 'even if we have been out for the day doing wall-to-wall activities or even if they have been at school all day. I know they are tired and deserve the downtime, but I become convinced it will just rot their brains. But the problem is, what will I do with them when they turn it off?' The prospect of a whole day with nothing planned seems to fill us with terror and we become convinced that time not taken up with construc-tive activity is time wasted because . . .

. . . the real reason we fill every waking moment of their young lives is that they must have an advantage, an edge over other children. Some sociologists have a theory that we pursue this inane timetable of extra-curricular activity because it is in some way making up for what was missing in our own youth.

Poppycock. It's all about improvement and being the best, isn't it? Getting one over on the Opposition. We don't seem to be satisfied unless every possible talent, however faint, is being exploited, and any possible hidden talents are being uncovered.

John shares the pressure: 'You find out that all these classes are going on at the weekend and gradually you

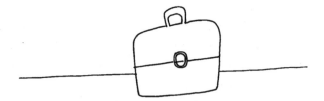

Lara found quality time for herself and
Millie at 4 a.m, before the gym.

think, Oh, maybe our children should be, you know, stretching themselves a bit more. Our children always have to be stretched – I don't know why! It's like some sort of medieval torture, but suddenly you feel a bit guilty that they're not doing ballet, football, fencing, architecture, glass blowing at the weekend and you start to sort of get swept up in this madness and start to go along to some of these things.'

First of all, of course, we have to improve the essential parts. We're not talking the basic coaching that is needed to give children a leg up to a good school, nor are we talking about sports activities for kids whose school curriculum (and lack of playing fields) allows for a negligible amount of PE.

Oh no, the schedule we refer to and to which we are slaves is the hysterical round of *improving* activities that will gives *us* the gold medal in the parenting Olympics.

Skills, skills, skills

Being tutored is like being coached but for the brain. How can we resist a sales pitch that promises 'the opportunity to realise their full potential . . . We can work to give your child the best chance of leading a happy and successful life . . .' Only the brave or certifiably insane would pass up the guarantee of a better skilled child – it would be negligent to really – and that's why so many sign up for after-school Kumon maths and English tutoring.

The whole ethos behind this, and other similar learning schemes, is the suggestion that a child's life will be more successful if they join up. Well, you can't be too caring, can you?

Gizella had a friend who wanted her son to be well rounded, 'so it wasn't enough that he was accomplished at sports and music and everything that he did at school, but he had to speak very well and so she took him to drama classes but the idea of drama at that age is very much, "ooh, let's be trees, and let's now be a river" or whatever – I mean it's meant to be very kind of creative and that's not the kind of drama she was after. She wanted her child to be able to not just speak well but to project well, as BBC broadcasters train to do. It wasn't enough that he had this extensive vocabulary and could spell all the words and could do his six times table. So in the end she actually got private tuition, once a week. He's three and a half.'

The weirder the better

The important thing is to choose an activity that has a whiff of the unusual about it. There are two reasons for this.

First, the more unique the activity, the more innovative and, frankly, inspired a parent you'll appear. Mandarin Chinese is a hot favourite, especially among children in university towns, and London, of course, where everything is available. Well, the Far East is such an emerging culture, you hear yourself say when quizzed about it by envious friends (envious because they didn't think of it first), and it will be so useful on Rory's CV. You, in turn, though, feel a flutter of panic when a friend says, 'Must dash,' and whisks her daughter off to coaching in some niche sport like racquets or real tennis. Then you are told another child is county standard, which sounds a terrifyingly high achievement and, in your panic at your own failure, you forget that there may actually not be that much competition to be county standard in croquet.

Of course we are all dedicated followers of whatever happens to be in fashion. Children's yoga – now there's an idea, especially when the literature says it 'stimulates children's imagination' *and* 'is a fun way to exercise' *and* 'helps them relax and learn to have balance in their lives'. Result: ticks all the boxes.

'I do remember trying to become one of those calm and beautiful-looking yoga mums and went for several weeks to this mother and baby yoga class,' says Fran. 'Harvey and I turned up for our weekly lesson in trying to look relaxed, lying on the floor of some woman's living room in Crouch End with a bunch of other women and babies. The hour for us was largely filled with me doing continual breast feeding and feeling most unrelaxed while everyone else managed to have such yogatastic babies that they had advanced to foot massages and chi baby breathing exercises. I finally decided I didn't have to keep putting Harvey and myself through this ordeal of smelly feet and chilly floorboards when the yoga teacher said, apologetically, that the session would have to end early as the yoga mats appeared to have some form of parasite, termites I think she said. I'd been trying to pluck up the courage to get off the whole treadmill. Oh, joy, the relief at not having to be a perfect yoga mummy.'

Circus skills is another fave. My kids are having fun, it says, and juggling is *so* good for cerebellum development – or so I read somewhere.

Second, the choice of odd options and niche sports gives your child the chance to shine at something because there is no competition. It's easy to boast about Henry's ability at the viol when he is the only one for a hundred square miles playing it. It's also a good way of getting him a place in the orchestra, which is always good for a boast because music sounds so brainy.

'I just know Hector is not a team player,' says Liz. 'He hates football – which I know is because he isn't very good at it – but it makes me feel a bit hopeless when all the other mothers in the playground are looking at the noticeboard and complaining in that oh-how-tiresome voice that their little darling is in the team on Saturday and they'll have to get them to the back of beyond. Oh, the sacrifices talent brings! So I suppose I consciously have looked for things he can do that will sound impressive and wipe the smug smiles off their faces.'

Oh, Liz. So it is she takes Hector along to fencing for an hour after school on Fridays. Touché!

The really determined among us find ourselves looking for sports that are *emerging* so, when the rest of the universe catches up, our progeny will have an edge. Have you thought of footvolley? Oh, you haven't? Well, it's going to be played during the 2012 Olympics at Horse-guards Parade, you know. George, explain the rules, will you . . . ?

	Greville	Jocasta
Monday 6.30-8.00am 5.00-7.00pm	Yoga Ski Club	Time with Mummy
Tuesday	Latin Coaching	Toddler tea Party - nb Brora (presents)
Wednesday	Swimming	Gymbonees
Thursday	Maths Coaching	Baby yoga
Friday	Trapeze	Mime Class
Saturday	Rest!	
Sunday	Museums part 2 (greater London)	Rest & time with Mummy

Of course a solitary activity is preferable, which cuts out synchronised swimming as an option – it involves relying too much on others. Archery would be okay, though you don't want people to think your child is a saddo, but it's so much nicer to spend the time talking to other parents while he is improving himself.

The Price of Success

And it is during that time when you talk to other parents, while your children are learning breast stroke or doing a David Beckham Football Skills Course, that you get the chance to share the pain of this punishing schedule.

'Isn't it exhausting,' you hear yourself sigh. 'I've got to take Izzy to ballet after this – she's practising for her grade 2 – then, while she's doing that, I'll drop Louis at tennis. He'll have to have a snack after all these lengths up and down the pool. Then tomorrow it's his drumming lesson of course, after his cello lesson and mini rugby the day after.' You see your companion's eyebrows rise in surprise and you go in for the kill. 'Oh, you don't do that? I seem to be going through petrol at an alarming rate and sometimes I think I might as well put a taxi sign on top of my car!' Because, the words hang in the air, my children are doing more than yours so will inevitably be *better*.

There is the awful worry in your head, of course, that Louis will never improve on the cello because he is never home long enough to practise.

The most popular after-school activity, though, is competitive boasting, as you find yourself trying to outdo other people about just how complicated your schedule is. Of course you've been juggling this tortuous regime since Bump 'n' Bounce when your children were toddlers, through Let's Make Music, Tumble Tots and then, when they were three, cookery classes. You were way ahead of Jamie Oliver. You're now hoping very much to get them to La Petite Ecole at Le Manoir aux Quat' Saisons, which seems a really fulfilling idea.

'It's some sort of hyperactive parenting,' says Marylin. 'Some of my pupils – all five and six – are doing activities after school four nights a week. And on the fifth evening they go out for tea. They come to school for a rest and I've had lots fall asleep in class.' The record we heard was a child doing nine activities in a week. We tried to talk to the parents but there was never anyone in to answer our calls.

There is always the danger of mutiny in the ranks – one friend's son told her it was a violation of his human rights to make him go to orchestra on a Saturday morning – and you can hear the resignation in their voices as they complain that they are fed up with doing homework in the back of the car, but what's the option if their sister doesn't finish trampolining until half past five and there's no time to get home?

Meanwhile the dog is in the boot, desperate for a walk. It will all be much easier in the summer when they have cricket nets and you can use the time to walk her round the park during the session.

You lean over to the glove compartment and pull out the contents – all easy-to-eat food like Pepperamis and Frubes (how did our parents cope without them?) – and offer them to the sulking child on the back seat. A picnic tea. What fun!

Totting up the Parent Points

While brownie points are something men get for putting out the bins or bringing tea in bed, parent points are awarded for Excellence in the Field of Schedule Juggling. You rarely see your spouse at weekends as you both head off in opposite directions to deliver offspring to football/rugby/swimming/golf/orchestra/theatre studies (or all six), and by Sunday night, once the whip has finished being cracked over homework, you both collapse in a heap and complain that the time has just *gone* and you've got nothing done. You don't have dinner parties any more because one of the children is at Saturday swimming galas until 9 p.m., and you can't afford to go out because you are getting through tyres and petrol like Jenson Button at Monza. Not to mention the cost of all these club memberships, and the equipment doesn't come cheap.

There's another danger too. One couple had two sons with different personalities and they never took two children out together. One would go to rugby with the father, one to museums with their mother. Result? Siblings with nothing in common at all.

The point we've missed, though, is that this relentless schedule-chasing is parenting by proxy. We're conveniently leaving the improving to someone else and, as we sit outside the piano teacher's house, flicking through a magazine or phoning our mothers on the mobile to complain how exhausting it all is, we omit to acknowledge to ourselves that this feeling of smug satisfaction of parenting well done comes as a result of someone else's skills and our cheque book.

Then there's parenting at even greater arm's length when it is the nanny who delivers and fetches the children.

'I get nannies who barely speak English delivering these children to my door,' says Caro, a cellist who gives private lessons, 'and I have barely any contact with the parents unless they phone to insist on knowing why their five-year-old isn't on grade eight. I'm exaggerating, but only about the children's ages. They might be nine or ten!'

There is something alarming about the fact that we are doing all this remotely while still congratulating ourselves on being good parents. In fact the more extreme we are in terms of the amount and type of activity, the better we think we are doing.

And what brings it to an end? The children themselves, who are either old enough to refuse point blank or who are so tired they can no longer function.

You get home one evening from hang-gliding, harpsichord and further nuclear physics, with just enough time to do homework, wash their hair and do their Kumon maths sheet, and your child is asleep on the back seat. 'They're waif-faced,' says John, 'and have bags under their eyes and you think, Actually, why don't we just give them Sunday off? I know, you can go to a museum or something.'

Ooops, there you go again.

'So, now you're in Butterflies.
Is that better than Snails?'

Glove Box Menus: a balanced diet

Fruit: Sunmaid sultanas, Winders and Jaffa Cakes

Dairy: Frubes, Cheese Strings and Cheddars

Carbohydrate: Dippas, Pringles

Protein: Pepperami, Dairylea Lunchables

Fibre: The cardboard it came in

Serve in a traffic jam with a warm Fruit Shoot, wet wipes and times tables.

9
Consumerism: Can I have one too, pleeeese? Can I?

Take a look around your house. Did you ever dream that having a child would result in so much clobber? It would be tempting to get a big bin liner and throw it all away, but how would we survive without the musical potty or the travel cot? Of course we all know a baby would be quite happy wrapped in swaddling clothes and laid in a manger, but aren't sippy cups sooo useful? And dishwasher-safe too!

Trouble is we're drowning in product these days but what a way to go! The retail opportunities are almost endless. Some of it we really, really need. Most of it we just really, really want. And of course, it's not real spending when you're buying it for them, is it?

Forty shopping weeks to go . . .

It all starts deliciously early. Pregnancy is now *the* prime retail opportunity. Now that mummies have to be yummy, you have to look the part, don't you? You can go with two opposing looks here. In one you can start drifting around in voluminous cambric smocks long before your

188

first midwife appointment. You could even get a T-shirt printed to announce the happy news. In the other (and slightly more irritating) you can do like the celebs and lay in stocks of designer black Lycra and just let that scrumptious little bump push its way into the open air, while claiming you haven't had to buy any maternity clothes. (Failing that an elastic band wrapped around the button of your jeans works for a while!)

These days even the traditionally boring purchases, like maternity bras, have been given the glamour treatment. Instead of the sturdy boulder holders that comprised the full range only ten years ago, you can now select maternity lingerie from Agent Provocateur and Elle McPherson. Not so much a balcony bra as a grandstand. Of course, nothing will ever make paper pants and nighttime pads an exciting purchase, but even stretch-mark prevention creams have been given a makeover, with emu oil, shea butter and a price tag to match. So that's you pretty much taken care of. But nine months is a long time – even longer than people spend on the waiting list for an Hermès Birkin bag, so the high-spending mamas need something to divert them. But don't worry, there's plenty more they can be buying before the baby actually arrives. And plenty of advice out there on how to spend their money.

Spending has never been so painless

For most of us, getting baby stuff is an excursion into uncharted territory. What do we need? Why? When? Back in the good old days, of course, our mums would dig out the stuff we had as babies and we'd use that until it fell apart. But that's not good enough any more. We're a generation who turn up our noses at the highchairs and cots she's been carefully storing in the attic all these years. We don't listen to our mothers' advice, because what do they know about children? So we get all our knowledge from TV and magazines – and they're all out to sell us something. The pressure's on to have new and to have the best. But with all the choice available now – did you realise there are over sixty-four three-wheeler buggies on the market? – where do we even start?

You've guessed it. There are people out there who will do it all for you. Like a fitted kitchen, you can now have a fitted nursery, designed, stylish, practical – and all taken care of by someone else. There are even bespoke baby shopping companies, conveniently located in quiet streets near the King's Road or in Primrose Hill, that will thoughtfully tell you what you need to buy in the way of equipment, from buggies, cots, linen to clothes, bathing products and gifts. You pay a joining or consultation fee – yes, really – and your 'nursery consultant' will take you through it, step by step, order it for you and have it all delivered. It will all be perfectly suited to your lifestyle and the statement you want your baby to make (other than 'waaaah'), because after all it's so difficult to choose between the FrostFrench papoose and the Bill Amberg baby sling. All you have to do is hand over your credit card – and they probably offer an epidural to take away the pain of that.

'Surely we can get an upgrade?'

Does my nappy look big in this?

When you're feeling a bit blobby but you have an over-whelming urge to shop for some lovely designer clothes in tiny sizes, what's easier? Go on a diet or start buying clothes for your children? Well, thank heaven the designers have seen sense and created baby ranges, or it'd be back to the grapefruit for most of us. High spenders can now dress their infants in Ralph Lauren, Gucci, Baby Dior, D&G, Young Versace and Kenzo; they can take their first steps in tiny Tods, and sleep the night away in their hand-made cherry wood cot, wearing Shanghai Tang silk pyjamas. For the super-rich, the sky's the limit. But even we ordinary mortals can get sucked in – albeit at a lower level.

'I don't think we went over the top,' says Lucy, looking back over her bank statements in horror. 'But we'd spent the best part of two grand before Thom was even born. It's absurd, because really a baby doesn't need much at all – I mean, look at how little most babies in the world have. But it all seemed so *vital* at the time.'

Didn't you feel, once you had a child, somehow different about your place in the world – simultaneously humbled and entitled? It has this weird effect on your wallet. We either resist the calling of the Visa and go and lie down in a darkened room until the urge passes, or we give in and go and buy a huge great car.

Clare chose the car option. It's the stamp of the yummy mummy.

'For the first time I feel vulnerable and exposed to the

world. Suddenly, my values have all changed and I want to protect my child so the best way to do that is to get a huge 4 x 4. So now we're elevated off the road, at a safe distance from the rest of the world. Of course, it's a gas-guzzler and I can't reverse in it, and it's ridiculously over-specified when we only have one child. Actually, it would be over-specified even if we had four. But it makes me feel *safer*. I've done the responsible parenting thing.'

Battle of the buggy

Funny how things sometimes come full circle. As a child, did you ride high in a stately Silver Cross pram, sheltered from the elements and snug as a bug? Or did you hang loose in one of those newfangled lightweight, high-speed Maclarens that could take corners on two wheels and folded up to nothing to slip into your mum's Renault 4?

Well, the tide of fashion has well and truly turned and supersize baby strollers are now the benchmark of chic baby transport. But why? The Silver Cross made sense when stay-at-home mums set the trends, and took long healthy walks to the shops and back. It even had a momentary return to popularity in the Diana Years. Then, when mobility became essential, and every mummy had a little run-around, the minimalist buggies were perfect for babies on the move. So why go back to huge unwieldy strollers when families are more mobile than ever?

It has to be a prestige thing, doesn't it? The rise and rise of the SUV stroller can be dated almost exactly to the guest appearance of a Bugaboo Frog on *Sex and the City*. Now they're everywhere. And so big! Jenny is apologetic about her huge buggy. 'I wish I hadn't bought it now. It's really very inconvenient and I'm always running over people's toes with it, or bashing their shins. Matt looks so tiny in it too. I only got it because I thought it would protect him but he rattles around in it like a dried pea. Oh, all right then, I admit I did get it because I'd seen pictures of celebs with it, so I thought it must be the best.'

'I don't like it,' says Jenny's mother, 'because I can't see Matthew at all when I'm pushing it. He could have fallen out for all I know. Or have a bee in his hair. A baby should be able to see his mother when they're out. It's ridiculous making fashion out of these things.'

Jenny's mother wouldn't be impressed at all, then, with a recent offering from Bugaboo: a limited-edition line of only 1,000, of which only 150 would ever be available in the UK. The price? A mere £1,100. 'Bugaboo is like the BMW of baby buggies,' the publicity gushes. 'In other words, your bambino will really know he or she has arrived in the world when you step out with your cutie in one of these state-of-the-art strollers . . . And then there's the added plus that you'll be turning heads wherever you go. If this is the bit that appeals most of all to you, then you'll love what comes next. Bugaboo have created a limited edition line with Bas, which takes the notion of pushchair posing to a whole new level.'

Pushchair posing? So that's what it's all about, and maybe that's why we have to buy a huge car – to fit the huge buggy in!

Toys: a serious business

'I was a thirty-eight-year-old, first-time mother,' explains Jess. 'I didn't have a network of friends with babies – all their kids were school age – so I didn't have anyone to ask. It was going to be my only shot at it, so I was desperate to get it right. When I look back on it, I was a sitting duck for advertisers. They must have seen me coming.'

So with this captive market of us vulnerable new parents, why do children's toys have to look so ghastly and tasteless? Sadly, because children seem to like them that way. Children are not known for their innate good taste so for those parents who have agonised over the interior décor of their homes, suddenly having all this plastic tat around is a big shock to the system. But then, we reason, why should we be so precious? It's the baby's home too and at least it's educational (in some obscure way we haven't worked out yet). When we get to that stage in our reasoning, we might as well raise the white flag and just hand over our credit cards to the nice people at Toys'R'Us.

Of course, occasionally we come across people who seem to have got a handle on this whole toy thing. Their calm woody homes contain a choice few calm woody toys and we think, That's how it should be. That's all I'll buy from now on, sensible toys from sustainable forests with vegetarian trees. That's until *their* little girl comes round to play and she flings herself at the revolting purple dinosaur that we were browbeaten into like a starving man on a loaf of bread and we think, Hmm.

When we were growing up, toys meant sensible things like wooden jigsaw puzzles, Animal Snap, sweet wholesome Sindy (not those whorish Bratz), chess and Meccano. A Sasha doll and Lego for the posh kids up the road. We got toys at Christmas or on our birthday, we looked after them and they lasted for years (unless you gave Sindy a bath, resulting in her head falling off). Playrooms didn't exist – they weren't needed, because all your toys fitted in a single wooden chest in your bedroom.

So it's all the more shocking the first time your child gets a surprisingly sophisticated plastic toy free with a fast food meal or inside a chocolate egg. And not at all surprising that kids have no interest in looking after their toys, or even picking them up off the floor or bringing them in from the garden. There will always be more and more. And the galling thing is, they're absolutely right.

The next fifteen years are going to be a nightmare of backache from picking up and tidying in our children's bedrooms, illuminated for a few years in the middle by the searing agony of stepping on Lego with bare feet. It culminates in them slamming the door and forbidding you to go in because you were careless enough to step on a CD, filed on the floor, while trying to manoeuvre the Dyson (but of course!) round the teetering piles of discarded clothes. At this stage, it's easier to give in and just fumigate the place once they leave for university – hopefully taking some of their possessions with them.

Consumers in training

'When I do the proper parent thing and take the kids to a museum or art gallery,' fumes Kris, 'all they want to do is get the cultural bit over and done with and go to the shop. And what do we get? What do we always get? A shiny pencil with the name of the place on it, a keyring – and a bloody great tantrum because I won't spring for anything else. I actually think they feel more comfortable with the shopping experience than they do with the educational one. They have more practice at shopping, don't they?'

There's no doubt our kids are very savvy consumers. They check their change, they pore over the Argos catalogue and spend hours mooching round the shops with their pals. For kids of ten and up, shopping is a form of entertainment. They probably even know what Statutory Rights are.

'My daughter and her friends live like middle-aged divorcées, meeting each other for coffee (well, hot chocolate) then spending the day trying on lip gloss and jewellery, looking at clothes they can't afford on their allowance,' muses Caroline. 'They're old before their time. At their age, I'd be out climbing trees or at home playing pretend games. They're almost scarily sophisticated but very naïve at the same time.'

Of course, there's a marketing term for the way our kids are. It's called 'age compression' or 'KGOY' (kids getting older younger) and it means that their childhood is truncated and they take on adult interests earlier than ever before. This means that eight-year-olds are craving mobile phones and if you haven't got an iPod by the time you're twelve, you daren't show your face on the street. 'Pester power' is no longer a cliché, it's a fact of life, and it's no coincidence that the expression that something is 'so *yesterday*' is so twenty-first century. Nothing is allowed to be 'old'. And if it is, it's pants. Everything has in-built obsolescence, doesn't it?

'I really dread my daughter's birthday coming round because I just don't know what to get her,' admits Teresa. 'She's going to be twelve and she's got everything she wants – apart from boobs. Bike, iPod, rollerblades, CD player. What's left? Only things she doesn't want, like game consoles. She's too young for jewellery, too old for toys, so what's left? More clothes? I wish they'd invent something new, so I could get it for her and she'd be the first of her friends to have it.'

Boys seem even more switched on to consumer trends than girls, according to Steph. 'My ten-year-old reads Jeremy Clarkson's column every Sunday. It's hard going for him, but he's desperate to know about cars so he sticks with it. When we go out, he knows every make and model. To tell you the truth, he's a bit of an anorak. And he's like that with trainers, mobile phones, music download software. How does he know this stuff?'

So if our kids have everything they need, why are we getting so worked up about finding something new for them? Haven't we given them enough already? Christmas panic sets in some time around September, according to Kevin. 'Christmas presents seem so pointless. I feel as if I'm trying to prove something. It's almost like I'm going through an exercise just to show how much I love them – do I love them £40 or £80 or even £270? And if I get an expensive present for one, does that mean I have to spend the same on the others too? I'm sure the perfect present is out there somewhere, and I'm damned if someone else is going to find it before me.'

Shame on you, Kevin, for breaking ranks from that unspoken don't-surrender parental cartel. Okay, so we all caved in and got our children those micro-scooters when they were all the rage – we probably crumbled from the pestering – but then, blow me, someone else goes and buys their little darling an electric one. They should be flogged as traitors – and for thinking of it first.

What not to (let your children) wear

Buying clothes for children is utter pleasure – when they're too young to have their own opinions. They look gorgeous in everything we put them in, we can indulge our daftest impulses and deck our daughters out in buttons and bows, our sons in cute little dungarees.

For the really imaginative, there's cashmere from top to tiny little toes (best keep them off the mashed banana though), organic cotton rompers and, wait for it, faux fur nappy covers. Whatever the fashion, it's like having your very own walking, talking doll, but regrettably it doesn't seem to last.

Ella sighs, 'My husband used to freak out at our credit card bill when the children were small but I couldn't resist anything! But I'm so glad I couldn't, because it was fun for me and now they're ten and twelve they just look ghastly all the time. If I get them clothes I like, they just refuse to wear them, so there's no point. They dress like . . . well, like chavs, frankly.'

Chavs is not the worst it could be either. Margot remembers collecting her daughter from a school disco: 'Fortunately, my daughter and her friends were all into those long cotton skirts – it was the tail end of the boho thing – and they all looked lovely. But there was this little girl there who couldn't have been more than nine, and she was up on the stage dancing, well gyrating like those girls on the rap videos, in a short denim skirt and a little crop top. Nobody knew where to look.'

The weird thing is for a brief spell – all too brief – we can dress like our little girls, thanks to the current quirk of fashion and the Boden catalogue. Don't you just love that trimmed cardigan and shift dress look, cropped trousers and floral T-shirt, with ballet pumps or flip-flops. If you're a teeny-weeny yummy mummy you and your daughter can both get your T-shirts from H&M children's department and be like twins!

'Oh, for the days when we were in sync and used to browse the catalogues together,' says Cathy, 'but that was long ago. Now she wants to look like – God help me – Paris Hilton.'

As a role model for young girls, Paris Hilton does leave something to be desired, but she features constantly in the pages of tween magazines, such as *Shout* (with its regular free gifts of make-up) and *Mizz*. A quick flick through the pages only serves to raise the blood pressure: Posh,

Charlotte Church, Lindsay Lohan and, incredibly, Pete Burns! Please, no!

Maggie is spluttering with indignation over this: 'Why do our pre-teen daughters need to know about a tattooed, cosmetically altered transvestite? Make-up tips? How to disguise five o'clock shadow? What message is *that* giving them about the world?'

Come back *Jackie* with your sweetly chaste fashion – all is forgiven.

Boys, once they manage to escape the indignity of having their mother as their stylist, are just as much victims of fashion (see later), but it's the grooming issue that makes us smile. Maggie's husband takes up the story: 'What his fourteen-year-old sister spends on make-up and perfume, our son easily spends on hair gel and Lynx deodorant. I think he must have seen the advert and be hoping for scantily clad girls to throw themselves at him. At his age, I'd cross the road to avoid a girl.'

And who's to blame for all this? Well, apart from us, of course, for giving in. The media, fair and square. We grew up with one commercial channel, and Channel 4 was only launched in 1982. Now there are an obscene number of channels all jostling for a piece of the advertising action. With tweens one of the fastest growing consumer markets, it's gloves off and not just on TV. Magazines and the Internet are just as keen to suck out your children's pocket money (and your savings). Ten-year-olds surf eBay to satisfy their insatiable appetites for consumer goods. We've trained them to be good little shoppers. Must have it all. Must have it now.

When Claudia asked for a Goldfish,
she meant the credit card.

And aren't they so savvy? It's like living with a mini-independent financial adviser. They watch TV so much of the time, our kids even know that if they go into debt someone will lend them the money to go on spending. 'We were chatting the other night about how we could afford a new car and Harry, our eight-year-old, suddenly piped up: "Just go to Ocean Finance." Now we're thinking of asking him to advise us about an ISA!'

Mobile madness

Those scares about brain tumours didn't last for long, did they? Now virtually every child at secondary school has a mobile phone – and they're trickling down to younger kids too – and all because of free upgrades. It makes perfect sense for the mobile phone companies to get more phones out there, because few of us have any qualms about handing on an old phone when we've got a nice new one. And it has introduced a whole new generation of eight-year-olds to the wonders of being constantly in touch. But hang on – when they're at primary school, they shouldn't really be out of adult supervision anyway. What's going on? Do eight-year-olds really need phones at all, let alone ones with streaming media?

'A six-year-old at my children's school had her own mobile phone,' seethes Gaby. 'Immediately all the other children wanted one. I could have killed her parents. Anyway, none of her friends have phones, but that doesn't stop her whipping it out every two seconds to check if she's been texted – is that a verb?'

If you're worried about any health dangers, there's always the Teddyfone, specially aimed at pre-schoolers with emissions much lower than those of conventional phones. Oh, and since it's for toddlers, it only has four buttons that you can pre-programme with approved contacts, and no screen either.

Excuse me, but what the hell is that all about? Under what circumstance could a toddler need a mobile phone? To call you from his cot to say he needs his nappy changing? Call me cynical but this wouldn't have anything to do with grooming ever younger kids to hop on the mobile bandwagon, would it perchance? Since many parents pay as much as £20 a month for their children's mobile bills, you've got to suspect underhand tactics.

But how about this? Mattel in the US, in conjunction with its content partner Single Touch Interactive, for example, launched the Barbie My Scene phone, aimed at girls between the ages of eight and fourteen. The phone is activated by parents, who can go to a designated website and list chores they want their children to perform to earn extra minutes. At the end of each month, parents can buy extra minutes if their children have behaved.

Surprise, surprise, children will then trade them in for the 'real thing' – they don't want to have stuff that looks . . . er, childish. Lee is resigned to coming a poor second to his technocratic son: 'I told him he could have my old phone when I trade up. But he keeps darting into the phone shop to look at the upgrades I could get, and I just know he's going to try to charm me out of the new one, so he can have it instead. And frankly, he'd make far more use of it than I do. I've got no idea about streaming media and uploading MP3 stuff. All I use my phone for is calls and the occasional text. The new one will be wasted on me. And I expect I'll let him have it, in the end. Grown-up toys are wasted on grown-ups.'

And this is exactly how our children have managed to get us where they want us. By growing up so fast that by the time they reach their early teens they are surpassing us in virtually every area of modern life – except in earning money – and money is really all they need us for now.

Beware. 'When I asked my soon-to-be-teenage daughter what she wanted for her birthday, she said a goldfish,' remembers Gary. 'How sweet, I thought. Until I realised she meant the credit card.'

Twenty things you've probably had in your house . . .

- *What to Expect When You're Expecting*
- *Toddler Taming* by Christopher Green
- Flashcards
- A GameBoy
- Inserts from a Kinder Egg
- An unfinished box of Cinnamon Grahams (minus free toy)
- Free toy from a cereal packet
- A receipt from the Rainforest Café
- *The Big Hungry Caterpillar*
- A Dorling Kindersley Eyewitness guide or CD-ROM
- A Burger King paper 'crown'
- An untouched SATs coaching book
- An unopened guide to activities for children around the UK

- Wax crayons
- An Early Learning Centre carrier bag
- *Guess How Much I Love You*
- Child-sized chairs
- A nightlight
- Anything that plays Brahms' *Lullaby*
- Fairy Non-Bio
- Gina Ford or Penelope Leach but not both (obviously)
- Ribena
- A baby gym
- A pencil from a museum gift shop
- A lollo ball
- A book by Steve Biddulph
- Playmobil
- A Thomas the Tank Engine pillow case
- Something with added omega 3
- Petit Filous
- A forehead thermometer

10

Teenagers: The Hormone Himalayas

It's 3 a.m., and you are in the kitchen on your third pot of tea, one hand poised over the malt whisky bottle, the other over your mobile phone. You didn't want to get one at all – heavens, you've survived your life this far without one – but that was before your children became teenagers.

Your ears strain for every noise that might be her boyfriend's car bringing her back from the party. Why hasn't she called? Perhaps she's in a bad area for coverage – a basement nightclub? Please, God, no. Perhaps she's run out of credit. Perhaps she's been run over.

Nobody warned us, did they, that parenting teenagers would be the single largest challenge of our lives. Now we understand why, when our children were younger and we moaned about things like bedtimes, the parents of teenagers just smiled knowingly and kept quiet. What is the wrangling about a nine or nine thirty bedtime curfew compared with the anxiety of them not coming home at all?

Now we also know what our parents meant by all the things they said (especially when we find ourselves saying the same things). They tried to warn us, but when you are faced with the arms crossed, sullen impenetrable face of a fourteen-year-old in a stand-off about whether or not she can go to a nightclub, suddenly the memory of your own teenage years disappears like the dawn mist.

Everything we ever said, every parenting plan we ever made, goes right out of the window as we struggle to keep up with an age group for whom 'because I say so' doesn't wash any more. Requests, which sometimes, if challenged, could be escalated into orders, used to be effective when they were smaller. Now orders are about the worst thing you can issue. Why should I? Whatever. D'ya think I'm bovered?

And if you lose your rag completely you know you have blown it, because there is nowhere else you can go.

If the madness of modern family life comes from the issue of control, then when they reach teenage we've lost it completely – in all senses! In the quieter moments, before we enter the theatre of war, we do remember our own childhoods. We did what we were told, didn't we? So where have we gone so wrong?

Problem number one: our children think we are hip. No, really. Our parents – raised by Edwardian parents themselves – listened to Radio 2 and Mantovani. We had to wear white socks with our sandals and dresses to go somewhere important. We, however, listen to Radio 1 while driving them to school (natch), buy the same fashions as our daughters, and can text with the best of 'em. Have you noticed how punk and the Brit sound of the eighties are making a comeback? Kids are downloading the Who, the Jam, Hendrix. Bands like the Arctic Monkeys would have fitted right in with Johnny Rotten. Instead of refusing to let them go to a rock concert, we find ourselves asking, Can you get me a ticket and can I borrow that CD?

Your daughter moots the idea of a tattoo and instead of flying off the handle, you wonder if you are too old for a discreet and tasteful little rose on your lower back. How can our children possibly know what the boundaries are if they are working out how to stop their mother borrowing their jeans and their dad from listening to their hiphop albums on his MP3 player?

Which brings us to problem number two and it's not unrelated to number one. Because we have so much more in common with our children, we are terrified of flexing our parenting muscles *in case they hate us*. Everything in our heads tells us to stand firm against unacceptable behaviour or demands. We've all read the advice that says teenagers and rebellion go together like a Big Mac and large fries, because it is all about learning to 'stand on their own two feet'. And yet and yet . . . when they scream at you that you are sad and old and they hate you and slam the door, you are racked with anxiety. How can you be 'sad'? You like Will Young.

It's that which makes us decide to go away for the night so they can have a 'few friends over for a bit of a party'. Who's to blame then when we get home, the house has been totalled, the cat is in the tumble drier and the neighbours have issued legal proceedings?

'My daughter has been grounded until July!' shrieks one yummy mummy. 'She's fifteen and she said she was only going to have a few friends round. Well, of course people found out and *she* couldn't cope with the gatecrashers. The mess! They even took the keys to the Maserati!'

What's so disappointing is that we thought we'd be so good at it, didn't we? We'd be understanding and in tune. We'd rolled a joint with a Rizla so we'd be on the same wavelength, wouldn't we? Not like our parents were. Oh, no. What we didn't realise is that the one thing teenagers hate but want is boundaries. They want parents not mates.

Problem three and not unrelated to problem two: there's less and less there for them to rebel against. The boundaries have dissolved when everything is there for the taking. There is every kind of sex and perversion you can imagine on the Internet; TV reality shows display adults they are supposed to respect in the most tacky light imaginable; the nine o'clock watershed means nothing when the contents of the programmes are trailed well before nine; the mothers of women who win *Big Brother* announce on the front of tabloid newspapers that they bought them sex toys when they were sixteen. What's left to discover?

'My eight-year-old seems perfectly at ease with the fact that Elton John has married a bloke,' says Lynn. 'He asked me the other day why celebrities married other celebrities and then, when he read about another big Hollywood wedding, I heard him say: "I wonder how long that one will last"!'

Problem four: we are far too busy with our own lives. 'There doesn't seem to be any strategic planning in being a parent these days,' says David, another teacher in the state sector. 'We are so busy juggling work and financial demands on us, even our own emotional issues, that we miss a lot of what is going on in our children's lives. What we don't realise, and indeed refuse to accept, is that in having children you have to make sacrifices. You have to be selfless. Parenting brings no rights – it's a life choice and brings responsibilities of selflessness with it.'

Crikey! That's something to think about when you are trying to sort out the latest crisis in your teenager's life. And what do you end up doing? The crisis has happened by the time you get to the scene and all you can do is put out the fire. Can't somebody out there help me?

No, but then we are parenting in a vacuum. Our parents may raise their eyebrows about the crazy decisions we make, but they have no idea what we are contending with and we have no previous examples to use as a guideline. Did they have to warn us about Rohypnol in our drinks and date rape? Did they have to discuss with us how a fatal virus is passed from person to person via anal sex? Did they have to explain to us why it is not right that you can see pictures of people having sex with animals on the PC in your own front room? We, however, find ourselves having incredible conversations about such things with our children. To paraphrase Talking Heads, how did we get here?

No wonder we look for help in our droves. You can't move for parenting know-it-alls, but their answers never quite match our questions.

Carly prided herself on sharing her
daughter's interests and tastes.

Keeping it between friends

In the category of teenage issues that have parents pacing the house in the wee small hours, the peer group may not seem like a priority, but it is. Despite the fact that we are meeting our kids on a leveller playing field than ever before, our influence is but nothing compared to that of their mates and other kids at school/on TV/ in Internet forums.

Teenagers today don't want to be different any more than they did when we were young. Remember the pain of wearing the wrong trainers? At worst we were square. How much worse to be a 'geek' or 'gay' or a 'loser'? The trouble is this peer group is now global, isn't it? What hope have you got when your child can go into a teen Internet chat room any time of the day or night and discover just how horrible a parent you are because someone in Seattle is still allowed to be sleepless till midnight?

Our kids *have* to watch the crap on TV because if they don't know what happened on *'Stenders* or *Strictly I'm a Pop Idol* last night then they will have nothing to talk to their friends about tomorrow, and, 'Francesca says like that I've *got* to be on MSN like *tonight* because she wants to tell me what's happening like about the *party* at Bianca's on Saturday.'

One withering look from them confirms your suspicion that they think you know nothing.

'I think peer pressure has always been there but the difference is children are more exposed to it than ever,' says Michael, a housemaster at a leading public school.

One advantage he has is he can keep an eye on kids in that dangerous after-school period which day schooling throws up. But what else are you supposed to do? Your kids will have to knock about with their mates because you don't get back from work until seven, and then there's the dinner to cook.

It's funny, isn't it, that we whinge about children not communicating with each other, yet they are probably communicating more than ever before. They ask each other out (and dump each other) by text; they bully by text and My Space and Bebo (come on, keep up, Lewis); they chat on web forums and MSN; they tell everyone which parties to gatecrash via the Internet. They can even talk to other players on the X-Box. Teenagers may not be able to write full words, but they are writing more words – no matter how abbrviatd – than they have since they sent letters to each other with the footman in Victorian times. Rabbit, rabbit, rabbit . . . and as they do so they are sharing how miserably deprived they are, how their mother is a witch and their dad is tight with their pocket money. They start to learn about rights – they've always got blasted rights (they've been threatening you with ChildLine since they could talk) – and quote the United Nations Convention on the Rights of the Child. With rights come responsibilities, you say, but something stops you laying down the law in case you are accused of infringing them. Heaven forbid.

You are running to keep up. Just when you thought you'd worked out the rules for something, the goalposts move. Oh, that's so last week.

But what they don't have is common sense. That still comes with age and experience.

And seems to leave you again when you become a parent.

Money and Mobiles

Perhaps the issues haven't changed, it's just how we handle them. But one thing that has changed is the ramifications of the mobile phone with teenagers simply because they didn't exist when we were their age. We weren't allowed to use the phone until after 6 p.m. because it was cheaper, and the phone was in the hall so everyone could hear your conversation anyway. Who would have imagined that you'd be able to take a picture, listen to music, go online, send an email – oh, and talk – on a phone while wandering along the road or hiding under your bedclothes!

Mobiles are not an accessory, they're a must have, an irritant – we've talked about them before – but where they have particular relevance with teenagers is that they enable plans to be made without your knowledge and they *cost money*. Money, mobiles, mobiles, money – the two are linked.

'My younger son, who's eleven, is on pay-as-you-go because he only has a phone in case he misses the bus from school,' says Gail. 'But what did I do with my fifteen-year-old daughter? I got her on a contract so if she got stuck somewhere she'd always be able to get hold of us. Next thing I know she's racked up £150 in one month on texts!'

And text they do – all day long. It's as if someone you are talking to is having a private conversation in front of you that you aren't part of. Beep beep. Beep beep. Out it comes from the pocket or the teensy handbag so they can see who's sent a message. They even take it out when it hasn't beeped to check they haven't missed anything. And what do the texts say? Lord only knows (and you probably wouldn't understand even if you read them, which of course you haven't . . .), but you can't help thinking it would be cheaper simply to dial the phone and speak to the other person. Lol. Cu l8ter.

Despite concerns regarding the side effects of mobile phone usage on children, it is us who are responsible for the increase. Ninety-five per cent of under-fourteen-year-olds have received their mobile phone from their parents. The average age when a UK child will now obtain their first mobile phone is down to just eight years. They need it in case there's an emergency in the unlikely event that they are ever allowed out on their own, don't they? Or at least that's what you grit your teeth and remind yourself as they download yet another polyphonic ring tone that is so irritating it makes you want to flush the damned thing down the loo.

And what does it matter if they use them to film each other slapping some poor unsuspecting passer-by? *So long as you know where they are.*

They are a double-edged sword, aren't they? We rationalise the decision to give our children one because of the security issue but, truth to tell, mobiles are an umbilicus. You can keep tabs on your children (when they

'Dad, are you downstairs? I'm nearly out
of credit, can you phone me back?'

choose to answer) and a 'Where the hell are you?' message will get to its destination, even if the little sod decides to ignore it. But have you heard? Several companies have launched a service that enables parents to monitor how their children use their mobile phones. Isn't that great? You will be able to track voice, text, video and picture messages and set limits on your children's calls. But best of all, the phone will also allow you to locate where your children are via a global positioning system. The power!

The only possible advantage of this phone addiction is that teenagers are apparently spending less on cigarettes so they can fund their mobile phone habit. But they won't be able to hold cigarettes soon, anyway, because of the RSI they'll get from all that texting.

Image, and the nip and tuck

Not sure our parents had to deal with this either: the growing demand for plastic surgery. Do you remember asking your mum if she'd mind stumping up for you to have a boob job, only the size of your breasts is interfering with your happiness and it is imperative that something is done? No, we don't either.

'Thousands of teenage girls are turning to plastic surgery in pursuit of bodily perfection,' goes a news report. 'Increasingly, it's seen as a totally acceptable way of improving their image – and more and more parents are willing to come up with the cash.'

There are no official statistics apparently – though over 40 per cent of teenagers say they'd like to have something done – but many cosmetic surgeons and clinics admit they are seeing greater numbers of young women under twenty asking for procedures ranging from bigger breasts to better noses. The average price of a 'boob job' is around £3,000. A nose op or liposuction slightly less, and though some teenagers go into debt to finance the surgery by taking out a bank loan or other credit, most of them have mummy or daddy to come up with the money.

It's one thing to want surgery to correct deformities or accident scars; quite another to see girls as young as eleven undergoing surgery for purely cosmetic reasons. But it isn't so much that teenage (and younger) girls are willing to go to such lengths to create the perfect image, it's the fact that many parents are willing to pay for it.

And why do they do it? Anything to make their princess happy. 'I know it's wrong and she's too young,' says Hailey about her daughter who's just sixteen. 'But I am terrified that if she doesn't have the tummy tuck she wants, she will be miserable.'

There seems to be such an obsession with the right to happiness that some schools are introducing courses on the pursuit of it as part of the curriculum. If we think that looking like a member of a girl band is the answer to all life's woes, then bring on the men in the white coats.

Drugs, booze and smoking . . . and money

There's some correlation between growing older and starting to read the *Daily Mail*. Against your better nature – well, you've been a *Guardian* reader since college, haven't you? – a headline about teenage excesses catches your eye and you find yourself agreeing with it. You are middle-aged, probably Middle England (even if you live in Hackney), and when it comes to drugs, drink and fags you are totally mystified.

'They are a massive problem,' says Michael, who confirms that it is not just among the richer children who are pupils at his school. Of course it doesn't help that they all seem to have so much disposable income.

'It really is a case of too much, much too young,' says Alice, who is coping with two teenagers. 'I can't believe how much money my children's friends have on them. Fifty pounds for a night out! With money like that burning a hole in your pocket you can afford a packet of fags, a few rounds of alcopops and change for an E. My children rail at me about how unfair it is, but holding back cash is the only control I have.'

That's music to Michael's ears – a parent who's exercising control! 'At school our boundaries are often different than at home – they are tighter. I wanted to suspend a boy for drinking and smoking, and his parents said, "But he does that at home." There are definitely parents who come home from a hard day at the office and light a spliff. What does that say to a child?'

'I wish I could have had parties like they do,' complains Clive. 'If I've got some extra cash in my pocket, then I'll bung some his way and tell him to have fun with it.' Thanks, Clive. Tempting though it is to live life through our children, that doesn't really help any.

School work, computers and er . . . money

As we all know, thanks to Margaret Thatcher, we can now climb the greasy pole. We can better ourselves regardless of where we come from. And if we didn't manage it then we still have another shot at it through our children. Isn't that reassuring?

That must explain why we put the pressure on them to get A*** for their GCSEs. Why we nag them about their coursework and then spend every evening tweaking it and adding to it so it's really really good. Competition is never as harsh as it is at the secondary level and it's partly thanks to parents who push from behind.

'Frankly, I chose his options for him,' says Giselle. 'He was in Neanderthal mode at the time and I said, why don't you do this and that and he just grunted. I just hope he doesn't throw it all back in my face afterwards.'

The scary part about this stage of their education is that suddenly you are not in the equation at school. Stay in touch, advise all the advisers. Keep up with what your children are doing. That's all very well, if you can get to the teachers, and you'll be lucky if you can get anything out of your children. Sometimes it comes as quite a surprise that they get any qualifications at all.

Secondary schools, to be honest, hate interference. We keep being told by other knowing parents, who are older and wiser, that we should just mind our own business and not get involved. You'll only be talked about in the staffroom. But it's impossible not to. Not being allowed to get involved means we've lost control completely.

Instead, you watch your children as they slump in front of the PC, which naturally is in their bedroom, because everyone else has one in their bedroom, and just hope to goodness they are doing what they are supposed to do. Then off they go on the school bus, shoes not done up properly, tie askew and hair fashionably ruffled, and you have no idea whether they have done homework to hand in or not. Until the report arrives.

Of course when it comes to the computer, you've even less clue what they are doing.

Shall we talk about computers? They're another thing, like mobile phones, that our parents never had to contend with. Let's face it, we're pretty new to them ourselves, and not only are our teenagers up to speed, they leave us behind on the starting blocks. You feel a bit like a superpower who knows the 'enemy' has more advanced weaponry and has already found ways to scupper yours. MSN – like texting – is a sort of private conversation that you have no part of and even throws up its own excluding language. GTG – got to go. POS – parent over shoulder. Of course, like we should, we invest in cyber-nanny software to restrict what they view, until the little bugger downloads a progam that bypasses everything else so they can browse bigknockers.com.

If only it were just big knockers though. 'I got all "well, it's like this, son" and tried to explain to him that I wasn't a prude,' says Steve, 'but how in our day we bought mucky magazines from the corner shop, but the newsagent was the first line of censorship. He'd draw the line at tits and bums. The Internet – well, it's all there, isn't it? Pervs, animals, even children; how in heaven's name can you keep up with the censorship?'

You can't. It's a damage-limitation exercise, fire-fighting at its most extreme. 'I hate it, that blasted box in the corner of the room,' screams Gillian. 'It seems to dominate their lives and sucks them in. And what do they expect you to do! First the screen's too small, then it doesn't have enough memory, then we need broadband. And now my daughter is nagging that she has to have a laptop because *everyone* takes notes in class on them at school and she needs to as well. Never mind the cost.'

Of course we have to eat our words when they go off on a gap year and we can email them when they are canoeing up the Amazon, in real time, and talk to them on Skype without it costing money. You see, Mum, computers are pretty cool really.

Clothes and . . . money

With teenagers the clothes issue is subtly different than just a consumer issue. This is another area where your control slowly slips away. Suddenly (and the term teenager applies here to anything over nine) they sense another area, like food, where they can flex their muscles. They can smell your frustration in the air and, boy, do they exploit it.

It's also another area where choice has become a rod for our own backs. Way back in the mists of time the choice was corduroy from Laura Ashley and something from M&S that didn't look too frumpy. Oh, yes and C&A.

Rebellious was black lipstick, but you wouldn't dare go the whole hog and do the punk look, though the New Romantic movement (Duran Duran and floppy fringes) was okay because you didn't think you looked *too* stupid (oh yeah?), but you could be sure your mother wouldn't wear it.

Now there's a whole high street of shops aimed at your daughter and which are okay with your daughter because you don't shop there – you know you'd look like mutton dressed as lamb (or at least, you *should* know that). Or she has the cheaper end of the designer labels, the prices for which still make you gasp.

'I thought I could fool my daughter with the designer range at Debenhams,' says a confused Lily, 'but she was having none of it. It wasn't the real thing apparently. She saved up for a pair of jeans for £180! Even her pants have to be some chic label – though I don't think it's chic to say chic any more, is it?'

Of course, there's the other temptation for them too: charity shop 'chic' which we conveniently forget we used to indulge in (remember the excitement of finding a granddad shirt for 50p?), but who wants their daughter looking like a hobo or a hooker?

Teenage boys are no better when it comes to sartorial terrorism. 'What's wrong with a pack of three T-shirts from Tesco?' wails one mother of two boys. 'Why does it have to be some over-priced surfing label – which racks up the price – when we live about as far from the sea as you can get? He has to have some snowboard or surfboard connection, when he's never done those things in his life!'

It makes you yearn for grunge when a ripped T-shirt and torn jeans were the height of cool.

Once the clothes are bought comes the dressing and, as any parent will vouch, this is a time-consuming process designed to drive you nuts. In fact so time-consuming that, with most girls, you can tell them it's time to leave for wherever, then go and mow the lawn, make bread, and have a cup of tea before they will emerge from the bathroom, fragrant and looking like Barbie (they all look like Barbie). And it is irrelevant where you are going – the supermarket or Stringfellows.

Then of course teenagers grow and they grow and they grow. Yes, yes, they always have but not quite at the rate we are now having to contend with. Stats show that our children are growing faster than any previous generation. Bob Hardy, the foot fitting manager at Clarks, says, 'Each range we do is getting bigger by a size or two. Our boys' shoes go up to a ten, girls' to a nine, and there are some twelve- and thirteen-year-olds who have grown out of our boys' ranges.' Then they have to wear adult shoes, which makes the whole problem worse because it increases the choice. Again.

Sons (or daughters) and Lovers

We purposely kept this little gem until last because, for once, this is a timeless issue and the emotions that surround it haven't really changed. The parents in Jane Austen went on about it: Elizabeth Bennett's dad wasn't too chuffed about Darcy. D.H. Lawrence took the subject to an almost incestuous level. Basically, once our children start having relationships, that last little vestige of them we had control over slips away. They fall in love, they start having sex with someone; they start having sex with someone before they fall in love – either way, it's the beginning of the end.

There are telltale signs. They go all secretive and coy. Phones (yeah, them again) get slipped out under the dinner table as they text Him or Her. Hair begins to be washed and deodorant used. Your favourite top disappears out of the cupboard (and that's just your son). You find yourself resorting to subterfuge as you use cleaning their room (you never did that before) as an excuse to try to find out details. Then they bring them home, with a casual 'Oh, this is Miles' as they slink off upstairs, and you are dying to find out where he lives, what his parents do. And you HATE yourself for it, because it is just the way your parents behaved when you were bringing home boys or girls.

The bit that *has* changed, though, is that they'll start having the sex earlier. 'I think those of us who were teenagers in the 1970s, we were the ones who changed things,' says Michael. 'We were cutting edge, so in many respects being a teenager now isn't that different – except when it comes to sex. Now there is barely a virgin doing A levels.' Wishful thinking we say. There's probably barely a virgin doing GCSEs.

Terry is blunter: 'The instant gratification that children demand these days seems to apply at the basest level. Waiting to lose your virginity doesn't have the same relevance it used to have – even we thought sixteen was worth holding out for, and even that was a little on the young side, but they can't wait at all. They have the mobile, the iPod, the TV and computer in their room. They probably have a double bed because we want them to have it all – so they think, Right, I'll have it all. They think they are all grown up, so now they want the sex.'

We did our best to dissuade them, didn't we? Of course we didn't want to come down all draconian and say, 'You are far too young to have sex, young lady,' because that's not the way we do things, is it? No, instead we sat down face to face, reminding ourselves about all the advice we'd read up on, and talked about 'mature relationships' and having sex in the context of a 'loving relationship', even how pleased we were that *we* waited, and they look at us but not at us, and we know it's gone in one ear and out the other.

So – damage limitation again – we fill the bathroom cabinet with condoms (and keep counting them), and keep our fingers and toes crossed, and hope they keep their legs the same way.

Of course an added complication is that we might also be dealing with a relationship issue. 'I'm a single mum,' says Fiona, 'and I struggle with the real double standard: trying to tell my daughter how to handle her relationships when I am trying to be drop dead gorgeous for my new boyfriend. I know I should be wearing prim clothes, like my mother did when I was trying to be a teenage vamp, and I find myself wearing short skirts and high boots because that's what he likes me to wear.'

So what do you tell them? With boys there's now the

added issue of being accused of rape. That's a tricky one that we don't remember being mentioned as our mother or father, pink with embarrassment, told us the facts of life in the car (always a good place for a talk, the car – no escape). And STIs need a mention too. They've forgotten about Aids – that's something that affects Africa – but chlamydia is a real concern. But why should they care – they're only fourteen.

'What I'm only just realising,' says Lucy, 'is that for all their posing and grown-up attitudes they are still very, very immature. They think they know everything because it's on TV, in the soaps, in the papers, but actually the fundamental messages aren't getting though. Pregnancy – and the risks of unprotected sex – for example get taught to them when they are ten or eleven, when they are still more interested in their bikes and the PlayStation, and then it isn't mentioned at the critical time, when they are about fifteen. And it's all very well teaching it as part of the National Curriculum, but they don't listen to anything else they are taught, so the last place they are going to learn about it is from a teacher.'

'I know in my heart,' says Anne, 'that I am older and wiser and I know better than they do, but when it comes to confronting the issues I have a crisis of confidence in my experience, my ability as a parent. Where's my conviction gone? It seems to disappear when I am faced with a "whatever, minger" attitude from my teenagers. I had the boundaries from my parents, and accepted them. Why am I too weak to put them in place for my own children? Why can't I just say "no"?'

Therein lies the madness of modern parenting.

And just as they come out the other end of childhood and become rational, sensible adults who you enjoy being with, what do they do? Leave home.

The Ten Most Irritating Things Teenagers Say:

- Calm down, dear. It's only a commercial
- Can you come and collect me?
- Yeah, whatever
- Can I borrow your car?
- I ran out of credit
- It's my life
- The party is at Gemma's house but we might go on somewhere else later . . .
- You're so *sad*
- Promise I'll pay you back
- Yeah, but nothing did happen, did it?

11
And then I woke up . . .

So what have we concluded out of all this? That, frankly, it's all terribly stressful. That it's all about being competitive, being the best and it's about other people. In fact, come to think of it, other people are the main problem. If it weren't for other people, the whole thing would be a piece of cake. We'd all procreate like rabbits and make quite a good job of it, but because, more than ever, we are judged by the quality of our families, we get in a tizzy about it: 'What *will* people *think*?!'

The difference now is *we* judge our own performance as people by our children too and worry ourselves into a frenzy about it. Parenting gets us tied up into the most awful knots that have us behaving in a totally different way than we did when we were childless, rational beings.

And to resort to cod psychology, these seem to be the factors:

Controlling Interests

Having children has far more of an effect on *our* lives than it did for our mothers' generation. Those were the days when *Good Housekeeping* was about good housekeeping, and they took pride in baking and washing in the new twin tub and hanging the terry nappies on the washing line to dance in the wind. They had the Pill, of course, but once they had gone up the aisle in damask silk they settled down and got on with the serious business of having babies. Some had jobs, some had good careers, but, when babies came along, it was okay to be a full-time mother. And, to get all sociological about it, likely as not their mother/aunt/granny lived up the road to help out and tell them how to do it. The difference is our mothers didn't want everything or believe they were entitled to it.

We, the Choice Generation, make babies part of a grand life-plan. We get the degree (in the days when a 2:1 meant something), find the career, find the alpha partner, buy the house in the right area, accessorise it, buy the car with the lowest mpg and emissions. Now, we decide, let's do the baby thing.

The result? We expect babies to fit into the balance of our lives. Everything else is within our control and we're damned if this new gadget is going to upset our perfectly ordered apple cart. We approach the whole thing as we might a job: we research it, we take it terribly seriously, we expect returns, and instinct gives way to something much less human. It's an R and D Project, an exercise in box ticking, an inter-personal solution.

Even worse, we've selected everything in our lives to say something about who we are and what we've achieved (the Dualit toaster, the Smeg fridge, the holiday in the Maldives), so it's obvious, isn't it? Our children must be part of our lifestyle statement. They must be clever, beautiful and accomplished. And preferably come with a lifetime guarantee.

The Curse of the Mummy

Pick your team: are you batting for the Full-Time Mothers or the Working Mothers? If we made the decision to put our years of over-education on the back burner (or away for good), then we have to make a career out of being a full-time mother, baking biscuits and making crafty things, to show we are doing it brilliantly. That should work to cover up our deep-seated fear that life is happening somewhere else, away from relentless round of toddler groups and bottom-wiping, and that our brains are slowly atrophying to the extent that we will never function as normal human beings again. FTMs criticise WMs as selfish and uncaring, and hope deep down that their children will come off the rails good and proper, at which point they will be able to sit back and crow about how 'important those early years are'.

WMs of course are well chronicled: permanently knackered, wrinkled before their time, riddled with guilt, and feeling quite nauseous from all that cake they are apparently having *and* eating. But, as they battle their way home from work, trying to put behind them the board-room struggles and focus on the brief quality-time they are about to impose on their children, they wonder which part of win-win they got wrong-wrong.

Social Engineering

Why is it that wanting the very best for our children brings out the very worst in us? The trouble is it goes a bit beyond just wanting the best, doesn't it? It's about wanting *better than you* and there are no depths to which we won't sink to achieve this. Whether it's sucking up to the teacher, getting our children tutored in Japanese, bribing the admissions secretary, booking the longest-haul holiday, having the biggest best everything, we can't seem to stop ourselves interfering.

It's made us into a pretty nasty bunch and nowhere is it more obvious than at school, the natural parenting habitat. 'When I look out on to the playground these days at picking-up time,' says Margaret, long-time primary teacher, 'I can see the parents as they were as children. In fact, it's like a mirror of the situation I have inside the classroom behind me. The same bullies, the same cliques, the same social manipulation.'

It becomes a bit like a game. You start on the first square and roll your dice. You scan the playground to find people you might be friends with and you form an alliance. Links of course are the only way to make friends, and it can be the most spurious connection. Ooh, she's got a Radley bag, she must be my type. It's like speed-dating by the hopscotch grid. And then shamelessly we try to force our children to socialise with the children of the people we want to get in with.

It can all get pretty nasty though if things get personal. Conflicts and tiffs between children were once sorted out in the classroom. Now they seem to escalate into slanging matches and nasty phone calls and that's just between the mothers. 'I've had to ban one woman from the playground until she calmed down,' remembers Betty, a head teacher. 'She picked so many fights I had no choice. Her daughter was as bad but at least I could put her on the naughty chair.'

Shouldn't we be able to talk to other parents about how hard it all is? Before we spawned we bored each other rigid about our love lives, didn't we, so why are we so reticent now? Do you detect a lack of adult solidarity here? It's hard to admit weakness and uncertainty to the very people we are competing against.

Lyn, experienced mother of older children, puts it succinctly: 'You only 'fess up when they are older. You can't admit you are failing while you are on the job.'

Mixed Media

Thinking about it now, we reckon we've been fairly lenient so far on the media but it has to take a big slice of the blame for creating the generation of Prozac Parents.

Issues, discussion, advice about parenting and how to do it/not to do it/to do it better are everywhere, and everywhere parents are being judged and found wanting. It's all based on half-baked parenting theories and lies, lies and statistics.

Google the words 'parenting advice' and there are over 27 million links. There are books on getting pregnant, thinking about getting pregnant, and thinking about thinking about getting pregnant. There's advice on being positive and not pushy, weaning without tears, getting them to sleep without committing violence, having the perfect relationship with teenagers and, while you are at it, being Nigella Lawson in the kitchen and John Prescott in the bedroom.

We live in a world where we have to find out how to bake a cake; how to plant a garden; how to train a dog; so why not how to raise a child? And it's more than that, it's how to raise the perfect child. There are guides on how to do it as a working mum, a stay-at-home mum and sometimes working sometimes staying-at-home mum.

Be under no illusion though: the aim here is not to reassure. It's to create anxiety that can only be allayed by buying the book, reading the article, getting the gadget, eating the vitamins. The overwhelming imperative is to sell product. The other myth we are fed (and we consume greedily) is the pap of celebrity parenting. We see this air-brushed image of effortless mother- and fatherhood in magazines like *Hello!* and *OK!*, *Heat* and the like, and it fuels our paranoia and our anxiety. 'I want to be like her,' we screech as we scan the picture of yummy mummy *du jour*, so we rush out to buy the stretch-mark cream she swears by, the buggy she takes round Central Park, the designer baseball cap her little (ridiculously named) darling is wearing. It's not unlike touching relics – we hope a little of her grace will rub off on us and our miserable lives – and we fail to see that behind this glossy veneer of celebrity lie the same puking babies, haemorrhoids and dissatisfaction that we feel. It's just hidden behind a pink Juicy Couture trackie.

Why do we swallow all this hype? Where on earth did we put our ability to make our own decisions? We must have thrown it out with the disposable nappies. (You didn't use those, did you? Haven't you heard about the planet?) Child-rearing has been going on since Fred and Wilma Flintstone, so why have we, the most highly educated generation ever, become so gullible? We are happy to hold forth on the subject of nuclear proliferation, but we'd rather die than admit we gave our baby a dummy.

The Pol Potty Regime

Following on from this tyranny of fear is the increased perception of danger and jeopardy – all that stuff about why playground games are being banned. And the result is a culture of general anxiety where everything is up for question. In 1971 eight out of ten eight-year-olds walked to school alone. Now fewer than one in ten does, because we've been cranked up to hysteria level that they will be abducted if they step outside the house. We run *Crime-watch* scenarios through our heads every time they are out of our sight. Now they are virtual prisoners in their own homes. Oops, then the media tells us they will get fat. Slap wrist, you shouldn't let them spend so much time on the computer; but hang on, they better had because, we are then told, they are falling behind on their basic curriculum skills. No wonder we are barking.

And then I woke up . . .

'Is that them or us?'

We become incapable of absorbing the statistics that in fact children are safer now than they have ever been, because they are hidden behind hysterical headlines and minute by minute of news analysis of the jeopardy that constantly threatens our children: murders, abductions, saturated fats. The media has found the chink in our parenting armour and, boy, does it put in the knife.

The Other Parent

And this is not just any old other parent. Another of those modern issues we have to deal with is the Ex-Parent. The one you used to parent with, but whom you now hand your children over to in the supermarket car park along with an overnight bag and a hiss about unpaid maintenance.

Breaking up is hard to do, but co-parenting when you are not only on a different hymn sheet but in a different house, is virtually impossible. It becomes an exercise in ante-upping. Like the Cold War (not a bad analogy), each side escalates the spoils and cranks up the propaganda against the enemy. One of you buys them a bike, the other makes it a moped. You let them have sweets; he responds with knickerbocker glories.

Even worse, you find yourself parenting someone quite unrelated to you or, conversely, your children can end up with another mother/father who's married to or has shacked up with your spouse. How can you hold any sway when there are three or four of you doing the parenting? Then of course they might have kids, and another set of grandparents and then the whole thing gets horribly complicated, especially at times like Christmas when one day to see the whole family simply isn't long enough. And you thought Father Christmas was busy.

Grand Designs

The last bastion of sanity is our parents, the grandparents, but the madness is we don't listen to them because we know better. Like the way antiques have gone out of fashion, so has the wisdom of their experience. They are the Queen Anne armoire of parenting, but we are the Philippe Starke chair: cutting edge and on the button and not terribly comfortable. But damn, we look good. They'd never have told us that though. Stop showing off, they'd have said when we were children, and Be quiet, I'm talking, dear.

Like those big fridges, self-esteem was something they only had in America in those days.

Anyway, what do our parents know? They must have had the odd concern about us – would we get scarlet fever or measles? Would the Russians bomb us? – but, come off it, they didn't have to cope with crucial decisions like which pull-up pants to use, did they?

Doesn't it drive you mad, though, the way they always tell you what to do; the way they question your lifestyle choices; the way they tell you that parenting should not be about diplomacy but about despotism (less Baby Whisperer and more Baby Doc); the way they poison your children with chocolate then roll their eyes when you show them the latest research from Sweden on how it might affect their fertility? And then, of course, they have to step in and pick up the pieces when your carefully ordered lifestyle falls apart because the nanny has walked out and you have to go to a conference in Frankfurt and pleeeese, Mum, can you have the children?

Of course they won't though, because they are having far too much fun learning the tango in Buenos Aires and spending your inheritance. How selfish is that?

So here's to our Admit-No-Blame Society: next time you find yourself getting your children to play their violin in front of visitors, or putting them on your answerphone message, or sticking a 'Baby on Board' label in the car window because it makes your car so much safer, you can just blame the parents. Yours.

What goes around comes around

And what will we end up with when our over-nurtured, over-protected and over-stimulated progeny reach the age of responsibility? Will they be gibbering wrecks of un-certainty who won't be able to sleep unless they are sung a lullaby, who will be morbidly obese from not being allowed to exercise in case they hurt themselves, and totally unmotivated because they have no idea about aspiration and the effort they need to put into life because you did their coursework for them?

Or will they be level-headed adults who will, like we did with hippydom and flower power, throw all our cock-eyed theories back in our faces and embrace a more laid-back form of child rearing? Will they take pity on us, the poor pilloried generation who were so besieged by advice we didn't know which way to turn, or will they do what we did? Yes, that's what they'll do. Blame it all on the parents. Theirs.

A Thank You Letter . . .*

It's been quite an eye-opener writing this book, and facing up to how we rate as parents. So it's been a comfort to know we are not the only ones who are fumbling our way through. Massive appreciation to all those people who have talked to us, on and off the record. They include Sue Margolis, Marilyn Bunce, Penny Wilson, Alan Beeton, Priscilla Chase, Jane Ross-Macdonald, Beth Elgood, Elaine Townshend, David Arthur, Sophie Campbell, Alison Purchon, Lyn Shone, John Simpson CBE, Steve Hayward, Deirdre Shields, Keith Adams, Helen Gunton, Lucy Horner, Fran Johnson, David Martin, Paula Byrne, Dr Sarah Thomson, Jackie Ciotkowski, Marie Rendall, Lucy Strauss, Peter Robertson, Clare Jervis, Doreen Massey, Dr Lisa Ford, Kate Newton, Sharon Walpole, Alex Fraser, Rachel Burn, Bob Hardy at Clarks, and of course those who wanted to remain anonymous for fear of reprisals! We know who you are! Hope we haven't forgotten anyone. Thanks also to Nicola Doherty, Sam Evans and all at Hodders, Nikki Melluish, Madonna Benjamin, Ian Denyer and all at Maverick TV, and everyone at RDF. Also of course Mary Pachnos, a doberman among agents.

AA and MS, 2006

* Remember them?